Cambridge Elements ≡

Elements in Religion and Violence
edited by
James R. Lewis
Wuhan University
Margo Kitts
Hawai'i Pacific University

VIOLENCE AND THE SIKHS

Arvind-Pal S. Mandair
University of Michigan

CAMBRIDGE
UNIVERSITY PRESS

CAMBRIDGE
UNIVERSITY PRESS

University Printing House, Cambridge CB2 8BS, United Kingdom

One Liberty Plaza, 20th Floor, New York, NY 10006, USA

477 Williamstown Road, Port Melbourne, VIC 3207, Australia

314–321, 3rd Floor, Plot 3, Splendor Forum, Jasola District Centre, New Delhi – 110025, India

103 Penang Road, #05–06/07, Visioncrest Commercial, Singapore 238467

Cambridge University Press is part of the University of Cambridge.

It furthers the University's mission by disseminating knowledge in the pursuit of education, learning, and research at the highest international levels of excellence.

www.cambridge.org
Information on this title: www.cambridge.org/9781108728218
DOI: 10.1017/9781108610353

© Arvind-Pal S. Mandair 2022

First published February 2022

A catalogue record for this publication is available from the British Library.

ISBN 978-1-108-72821-8 Paperback
ISSN 2397-9496 (online)
ISSN 2514-3786 (print)

Violence and the Sikhs

Elements in Religion and Violence

DOI: 10.1017/9781108610353
First published online: March 2022

Arvind-Pal S. Mandair
University of Michigan

Author for correspondence: Arvind-Pal S. Mandair, amandair@umich.edu

ABSTRACT: *Violence and the Sikhs* interrogates conventional typologies of violence and nonviolence in Sikhism by rethinking that religion's dominant narrative as a deviation from the ostensibly original pacifist-religious intentions and practices of its founders. This Element highlights competing logics of violence drawn from primary sources of Sikh literature, thereby complicating our understanding of the relationship between spirituality and violence, connecting it to issues of sovereignty and the relationship between Sikhism and the state during the five centuries of its history. By cultivating a nonoppositional understanding of violence and spirituality, this Element provides an innovative method for interpreting events of "religious violence." In doing so, it provides a novel perspective on familiar themes such as martyrdom, martial race theory, warfare, and (post)colonial conflicts in the Sikh context.

KEYWORDS: violence, nonviolence, Sikhism, spirituality, martyrdom, conflict

ISBNs: 9781108728218 (PB), 9781108610353 (OC)
ISSNs: 2397-9496 (online), 2514-3786 (print)

Contents

1 Representing Violence

For many who have been drawn to the study of Sikhs and Sikhism, the prevalence of external observable violence – whether in the form of its martial tradition, the centrality of the "spiritual warrior" (*sant sipāhī*) motif, the veneration of martyrs and martyrdom, proclivities towards antistate resistance in the form of guerilla warfare well into the late twentieth century, or its associations with terrorism and state insurgency – has provided a powerful source of fascination. Such fascination is not surprising given that Sikh history is replete with instances of violence that begin as early as the period of the later Sikh Gurus, and continue all the way into the last decades of the twentieth century. Ironically, it is the "spectacle" of violence associated with Sikhs and Sikh politics in the 1980s that attracted scholarly attention in the first place and brought Sikhism to world attention.

Notable examples of "spectacular" violence involving Sikh organizations and individuals in high-profile events of political violence, especially during the 1980s, include the following: (i) nonviolent mass protests organized by the main Sikh political party, the Akali Dal, against the ruling Congress Party's imposition of Emergency in 1975, which proved instrumental in ousting Indian Prime Minister Indira Gandhi from power in 1977; (ii) a spate of bombings, hijackings, and political assassinations of police officials and public notaries linked to Congress or the Hindu right; (iii) from 1980–83, the rise of Sikh militant groups inspired by the charismatic cleric Sant Jarnail Singh Bhindranwale, targeting law enforcement agencies and politicians; (iv) in early 1984, the occupation of the Akal Takht building located in the Golden Temple complex, the central pilgrimage site of Sikhism, by Bhindranwale and his supporters; (v) between June 5 and 7 of the same year, under the orders of Prime Minister Gandhi, the Indian Army's military operation to oust Bhindranwale resulted in the massacre of around 3,000 people, including Indian soldiers, innocent pilgrims, and Bhindranwale himself; (vi) in October 1984, the assassination of Indira Gandhi, followed by three days of anti-Sikh pogroms in Delhi and throughout India, resulting in the massacre of over 5,000 Sikhs; (vii) the rise of a major Sikh insurgency in India supported by transnational diasporic networks fighting for the establishment of an independent Sikh state called

Khalistan; (viii) the blowing up of Air India flight 182, killing 336 passengers off the coast of Ireland – an act allegedly perpetrated by Sikh militants, although there has been increasing speculation that the operation may have been orchestrated by Indian intelligence agencies; (ix) a decade of state-sponsored terrorism by Indian paramilitary forces to suppress the Sikh insurgency, resulting in routine disappearances, tortures, and extra-judicial executions of tens of thousands of combatant and noncombatant Sikhs.

The above list represents a few among hundreds of catalogued events of political violence involving Sikhs. Between 1980 and 1992, these instances of violence were closely monitored by news media around the world that, by and large, followed a trend set by Indian state media of profiling turbaned Sikhs as religious fanatics. Further, Sikhism was portrayed as a religious system with a proclivity towards both violence and the disruption of liberal democratic law.

In line with this, some academic scholars reestablished a resilient narrative representing two opposing versions of Sikhism precariously situated between peace and violence. This narrative centered around a "peaceful Sikhism" inclined towards its founding figure Guru Nānak, depicted in this narrative as a pacifist, purely spiritual person who did not get involved in the politics of the day. This is juxtaposed against a "violent Sikhism" that, according to the very same narrative, follows the example of later Gurus who attracted unruly elements into the movement and became involved in worldly politics and violence against the Mughal state.

Since the late 1990s scholars have paid closer attention to the underlying causes of the Sikh–India conflict, resulting in a more nuanced picture of Sikh involvement in violence. In spite of extensive research on this topic, however, the structural dualism of the narrative distinguishing "peaceful" from "violent" Sikhism has not only further embedded itself into contemporary representations of Sikhism, but makes two key assumptions about the nature of violence itself. First, that observable (external) violence is the only kind of violence there is; that violence consists essentially of an empirical, therefore recordable/datable, event in historical time; and that this empirical event is all we need to understand the nature of violence in the study of Sikhism. Second, that violence is essentially a fall or deviation from its originally nonviolent religio-spiritual or devotional state. Reproduced in encyclopedias, textbooks, academic research, TV documentaries, world religions textbooks, and the Internet, the dualist narrative not only provides a simplistic explanation for the transition from pacifism to violence, but also makes a fundamental distinction between two forms of Sikhism – its "authentic" or properly religious form, versus the "inauthentic" (because deviant) form that involves itself with violence.

Closer scrutiny reveals several problems with this narrative. Once it is structurally established, it is a very short step to assuming that Sikhs are innately violent or that Sikhism is inherently prone to violent insurrection against the rule of any state. This view was actively propagated by sectors of the Indian media and state apparatus during the 1980s. Second, the dualist narrative is significantly at odds with the philosophical teachings of the Sikh Gurus (*gurmat*) arising from the central textual sources of Sikh tradition, particularly its scripture. These writings present a rich but qualitatively different understanding and conceptualization of violence, which, at the very least, complicates the peace–violence binary. Indeed, modern representations of Sikhism – both academic and traditionalist – tell us little, if anything, either about *the nature of violence* as such, or about the *relationship* between religion and violence, except that violence is secondary to pacifism, a deviation from religion.

The overarching aim of this Element is to present a more holistic understanding of violence in Sikhism. To do this, it is necessary to complicate the conventional modern image of violence as limited to observable, external events, by bringing it into productive conversation with an internal violence that can be gleaned directly from the writings of the Sikh Gurus (Section 2).

The conventional perspective on violence is reflected in a sizeable body of publications in modern Sikh studies that develop an image of violence in the Sikh context based on texts known as the *gurbilās*. These texts (lit. "splendor of the guru") are basically hagiographical narratives about the heroic military exploits of the sixth and tenth Gurus, stressing their role as warrior-saints. Much of the *gurbilās* literature appeared between the late eighteenth and early nineteenth centuries, although it draws inspiration from early eighteenth-century works such as Sainapati's *Gur Sōbha* and *Bachitar Nātak*. To varying degrees, almost all modern publications on Sikh violence (see Section 3) follow a suggestion by the influential historian of Sikhism, W. H. McLeod, that as "the form and dominant philosophy of the Panth changed, so too did its religious perceptions and the literature which gave them expression" (McLeod, 1984: 11).

At the heart of this thesis, which was developed by McLeod in later publications, yet rarely subjected to critical scrutiny, are two key assumptions. First, that the "dominant philosophy of the Panth" is a pacifist devotionalism supposedly espoused by Guru Nānak's praxis and teaching. Second, that the engagement in violent conflict on the part of the later Sikh gurus and the evolving Sikh community represents a fundamental deviation from Guru Nānak's teaching – which is to say that violence has nothing to do with Guru Nānak's teaching.

This Element challenges this thesis on the grounds that: (i) it fundamentally misinterprets the "dominant philosophy" or teaching of Guru Nānak (and therefore of the Panth); and (ii) that it never questions the *concept* of violence itself. In fact, the thesis propagates a concept of violence drawn less from Sikh tradition than from the modern tradition of liberal secular philosophy, which views the distinction between pacifism (as the essence of religion) and violence (as essentially nonreligious) as normative. I offer a different interpretation in this Element.

While changes in political circumstances led to violent conflict, which has been observed and recorded in memory and history, the "dominant philosophy of the Panth" – whose primary source is *gurbāṇī*, or Sikh scripture, specifically the writings of Guru Nānak – *did not change*. It has remained relatively constant. Indeed, *gurbāṇī* is not only the primary source of inspiration for the later *gurbilās* genre, but the concepts of *gurbāṇī* provide the religio-philosophical premise for the concept of violence in the *gurbilās* texts.

If, as I argue, a liberal image of violence is uncritically adopted by much of the modern scholarship on Sikh violence, is it possible to extract an alternative concept of violence from the Gurus? Indeed, what does this alternative concept of violence tell us about the *nature of violence*, or about relations between Sikhs/Sikhism and the state? And, if a radically different understanding of violence does indeed exist, how do we speak, think, and write about it in relation to the conventional image of violence? Can both approaches to violence exist side by side?

Probing the Pacifism–Violence Binary

We can start by digging a little more deeply into the origins of the pacifism–violence binary. Scholars in the field of critical religion studies such as William Cavanaugh suggest that it can be traced to two related sources. On the one hand, to the creation myth invented by the modern secular state to justify marginalization of religious loyalties in order for the state to secure a legal "monopoly on the means of violence" (Cavanaugh, 2008: 123). And, on the other hand, to a version of this creation myth that was transplanted into late eighteenth- and nineteenth-century colonial writings about the various "religions" encountered by European administrators, scholars, and travelers (Cavanaugh, 2008: 85–122). The colonial writings on or about Sikhs and Sikhism are exemplary of this trend because the pacifism–violence binary is certainly not to be found in the writings of the Sikh Gurus themselves. Yet it was seamlessly carried over from colonial writings into the modern academic discourse on Sikhism produced in the last decades of the twentieth century.

For example, the dominant narrative about Sikhism and violence first appeared in John Malcolm's *Sketch of the Sikhs* (Malcolm, 1812). This mainly ethnographic text was composed by a military employee of the East India Company charged with gathering surveillance material on the Sikhs with whom he had direct contact at the height of their power. Malcolm's thesis on Sikh violence found its way into almost every work on Sikhism over the next two centuries. A more refined version can be found 200 years later in the writings of W. H. McLeod, notably in his lucid text *Sikhism* (McLeod, 1998).

Between Malcolm's "Sketch" (1812) and McLeod's *Sikhism* (1998), other than the accumulation of more precise facts, what remains unchanged in this narrative are the following assumptions: (i) that Sikhism begins with Guru Nānak who was a pacifist, and whose concerns were "explicitly religious" (McLeod, 1998: 10); (ii) the transition from this pacifist origin towards militant violence is contrary to Nānak's doctrine and represents a deviation from authentic/normative Sikhism to a deviant, inauthentic state; and (iii) violence is perpetrated by secondary actors seduced by worldly politics who deviate from the essential religiosity of Guru Nānak's doctrine and thereby cause the Panth to transform its essential identity.

Over the last two centuries, this liberal narrative of violence was internalized by colonial elites and continues to be enunciated by Sikhs today. Two examples of this internalization include the Sikh journalist and historian Khushwant Singh, and contemporary Sikh advocacy groups in the USA. At around the same time that McLeod's *Sikhism* was published (1998), the BBC released a documentary called *The Sikhs* to mark the tercentenary of the creation of the Khālsā – the religious military order of the "warrior-saints." Among the interviewees in the BBC documentary was Khushwant Singh, who explained the transformation of Sikhism by likening it to the proclivity of Christian Crusaders for militant violence in the name of religion:

> It's the same with Sikhism. It began as a pacifist faith [Nānak], . . . changed to a militant faith [Khālsā of Guru Gobind Singh], . . . and we keep the two sides together.
>
> (Singh, 1999)

The militant faith or Khālsā is further described as a "kind of hot-house existence" as opposed to the apparently less excitable version of Guru Nānak.

A rather different example, but one that follows the same pattern, can be gauged from the responses of American Sikhs and especially Sikh advocacy groups in the post-9/11 period. Following the killings of a number of Sikhs by white supremacists, Sikh advocacy groups were given airtime on mainstream American media networks to explain the nature of Sikhism, and who Sikhs are, to an American public influenced by the toxic atmosphere of Islamophobia. Their response started by repeating the customary mantra that Sikhism is a peaceful religion, and that it is essentially akin to the Christianity that Americans understand and are familiar with, that "Sikhism is as American as apple pie!" one advocate mentioned (Singh, 2012). Conveniently downplayed in such enunciations is the long history of Sikh involvement with violence, not to mention the relatively recent episodes of violent Sikh insurgencies within the modern Indian state (supported by Sikhs in the Western diaspora), and the hijacking of popular Sikh discourse by those on the fringes of the community.

The point here is *not* that such responses are true or false. Rather, it is that both narrative and response echo a modern liberal understanding about the relationship between religion and violence in which the state is assumed to be the arbiter of peace or nonviolence and provides a foundational definition for what counts as violence and equally for what counts as religion (Cavanaugh, 2008, 2017). Far from being a neutral entity the state plays a crucial role in defining not only the *meaning of religion* but in equal measure the *meaning of violence*, even as the defining process remains invisible (Asad, 2007: 7–91). Thus the meaning of violence, far from being objective or universal in essence, is predetermined by a "State-form."[1]

Briefly, the term State-form refers to any abstract entity characterizable as a state irrespective of historical, cultural, or civilizational differences between actual states. This commonality is best described in terms of key processes that define the state's functions, such as the establishment of a dominant regime of representation able to control meaning-making by imposing its own system of signification on all forms of social life, thereby controlling the ways individuals connect with one another within a society. In this sense, the State-form is essentially a machine that recodes the way we think, thereby impacting everyday life and capturing the very means by which individuals can form social relations and the way societies interact with one another. As scholars have increasingly recognized, the ideology of liberal secularism as it emerged in modern Europe is exemplary of the State-form's ability to recode our ways of thinking and living (Fitzgerald, 2015: 248–79). Perhaps the best example is the way in which the modern liberal European state overcoded the signifier "religion" by elevating it to the status of a master signifier. Such recoding of "religion" enabled the

---

[1] I adopt the term "State-form" from Deleuze and Guattari's use of the term in *A Thousand Plateaus* (1987). Their usage in turn follows Pierre Clastres' depiction of the state as essentially a means of capture.

emerging modern state to monopolize the meaning and definition of terms such as "violence."

The upshot of this is clear: if the terms "religion" and "violence" do not have the same meaning at all times and in all cultures, it becomes necessary to adopt a more critical and reflexive stance *towards the mode of thought* in which violence is framed. How, and in what sense, was this conventional meaning of violence framed? What was and continues to be invested in such a framing?

In the last two decades, such questions have been vigorously debated by scholars working at the intersection of critical theory and the study of religion. In the next section, I look at how such scholarship has shed light on the ways in which we have been conditioned to think dogmatically about violence. In turn, this dogma about the meaning of violence – the assumption about *what violence is* – has affected how non-Western cultures are represented in a global context. It is this broad caricaturing of violence in non-Western contexts that opens up the central task of this Element, which is to explore the ways in which the philosophical teachings of the Sikh Gurus (*gurmat*) have conceptualized and practiced a sense of violence that is qualitatively different from the way violence is understood by liberal secular moderns. If we can unframe the conventional notion of violence, this might give us a better idea of what is going on, not only in the key textual sources of Sikh tradition (which suggest a very different way of understanding violence), but in the scholarly understanding of religion and violence in general. By unsettling the dogmatic image of violence imposed by secular liberalism, it is possible to explore alternative concepts arising from Sikh textual sources that have a direct and indirect bearing on the practice and understanding of violence. This will be the task of Sections 2 and 3 in the Element.

The "Dogmatic Image" of Violence

In the past two decades, growing numbers of scholars in the humanities and social sciences have noted that something is awry with the way we perceive (and are expected to perceive) violence. The idea that we all know what violence is, especially when we see or experience it directly, is now beginning to be recognized as a conventional wisdom. Critical thinkers have long suggested that the violence we all assume to be a universal phenomenon, because of its sheer visibility, is based on an uncritical thought process – effectively, an assumption – about *what violence is*, thus creating an "image of thought" that has become *dogmatic* (Deleuze, 1994: 130–8).

Ultimately, this dogmatic form of thought, on the basis of which we make assumptions about what is, or is not, violent, stems from a dualistic mode of knowledge and knowing that divides reality into true versus apparent worlds.[2] The true world corresponds to what is permanent and fixed, while the apparent (and, by implication, *false*) world is the one that is subject to all manner of change. The dogmatic image of thought is therefore one that has an affinity towards permanence as the underpinning condition of what counts as truth or reality. Accordingly, permanence or eternity is assumed to be the ontological condition of peace, which naturally renders any change or becoming as a violation of eternity/permanence. Hence violence per se is associated with change – and this is perfectly plausible because change is supposedly evident to us all. In this way, our perception of violence and judgment of it *in terms of what seems most visible about it*, and the fact that we push to the back of our minds what is *not so visible* about it, constitutes a value judgement.[3]

In his ruminations on violence, Slavoj Žižek shows how to step away from the "fascinating lure" exerted by this dogmatic image of violence (Žižek, 2008: 1). He suggests that the visible violence we identify as empirical violence and which the media bombards us with, is in fact part of a "triumvirate" of different forms of violence. There is, first, the obvious form of violence, which he calls "subjective violence" – the kind that is most easily empirically identifiable – including religious terrorism, international

[2] This is the mode of knowing or epistemology that dominates Western thought from Plato to Kant. It produces the subject–object dichotomy central to "representation," which is effectively what Deleuze means by the "dogmatic image of thought."

[3] A version of this can be found in Grace Jantzen, *Foundations of Violence*, London: Routledge, 2004.

conflict, and civil unrest (Žižek, 2008: 2). This is the violence that fascinates us because it is directly visible and "performed by a clearly identifiable agent" (Žižek, 2008: 1). As critical thinkers, we need to identify the background machinery that generates this visibility and our attraction towards it. By doing this, it is possible to reveal a deeper violence that underpins our very efforts to replace overt visible violence with peacemaking.

Žižek refers to this deeper violence as "objective violence," of which there are two kinds. There is, in the first place, a "symbolic violence." By symbolic violence, Žižek refers not only to the more obvious kind of violence that pervades intentionality associated with our everyday and habitual forms of speech, and best illustrated by things such as hate speech, which incites others to enact physical violence with a view to produce social domination. Symbolic violence also includes a more fundamental violence that pertains to language *as such*, to the way that language has the ability to impose a certain "universe of meaning." Second, apart from symbolic violence, there is what he calls "systemic" violence, which stems from the "smooth functioning of our economic and political systems" (Žižek, 2008: 1–2).

The problem is, however, that it is not possible to perceive the dualistic framework – subjective/objective – from the same standpoint. As Žižek maintains, this is because "subjective violence is experienced as such against the background of a *non-violent zero level*. It is seen as a *perturbation of the 'normal' peaceful state* of things. However, objective violence is precisely the violence inherent to this 'normal' state of things. Objective violence is invisible because it sustains the very zero-level standard against which we perceive something as subjectively violent" (Žižek, 2008: 2, emphasis added; see also Mandair, 2011: 62–84).

Žižek's characterization of "systemic" violence in terms of the "smooth functioning of our economic and political systems" is perhaps better understood in terms of Deleuze and Guattari's argument for the essential proximity between State-form and the dogmatic image of thought. For Deleuze and Guattari, the State-form is an apparatus of capture. It is a "system which conditions its surroundings so as to perpetuate and enhance its own existence … bringing the 'outside' to the 'inside'." It is, therefore, the form that "appears as pre-accomplished and self-presupposing" (Deleuze &

Guattari, 1988: 448–9). Part of this pre-accomplishment is its self-presupposition as keeper of the normal peaceful state of affairs in a world that would otherwise be rent asunder by violent chaotic forces. To say that this objective violence remains invisible is to say that the State-form directs attention away from the real forces that give rise to its image as a peacekeeper or "non-violent zero level." In other words, the State-form consists precisely in the image of thought that it both imposes and sanctions as correct or as truth.

Although Žižek and Deleuze refer to it only obliquely, this idea of the State-form as an objective "non-violent zero level," and the framing of the very meaning of violence into its conventional form, resonates well with Cavanaugh's depiction of the ongoing separation of church and state following the Treaty of Westphalia. Cavanaugh argues that it can be seen in the kinds of creation myth that the ideologues of secular liberalism or humanism devised to bring an end to the so-called "wars of religion" by effecting a seamless transfer of power and popular loyalty from church to state (Cavanaugh, 2017: 589–97). In order to account for the transition of power from Christianity to the modern secular state, administrators and ideologues devised the myth that the secular state was necessary to save us from the chaos resulting from wars of religion and ensure a lasting peace for the prosperity of the people. The myth involved much more than simply saying that, through the exercise of rationality, "violent religion" gives way to a "peaceful secular state." It involved the subterfuge that a "peaceful secular state" did not evolve in progressive stages. Evidence of its history had to be erased, giving the impression that it was born *ex nihilo*.

To make the transition believable it was necessary to divest religion of its divinity and transfer it to the state, while giving the impression that the latter is a humanistic entity. To do this, state ideologues took the ancient metaphysical dualism between the true world/apparent worlds, permanence/change, peace/violence described above, and weaved it into an ontological distinction between religion and state, but one in which religion and state reverse their essential characteristics. In the reversal, religion is redefined in terms of God's essential characteristics (immutability, eternal stasis = infinite peace) while the state becomes the keeper of this characteristic of infinite peace or eternal stasis. The reversal itself is achieved through the artifice of historicism, giving the impression not only that we all occupy the same temporal frame (*saeculum*), [4] but that there is simply no other temporal frame that exists. Moreover, within this one and only temporal frame (*saeculum*), any form of life designated by the state as "religion" is distanced from the present, imprisoned in the depths of history, and effectively divested of agency for change and becoming, which now becomes the prerogative of the modern state.

Thus the state is both able to change and hold the definition of religion as peace (= non-change). Sedentarity now becomes the essential characteristic of the state – that which it is given to protect at all cost – even as it evolves historically. The state assumes objectivity while any entity that challenges the new temporal order ("religion," for example) is regarded as entirely subjective. Once this ontological distinction is instituted into law, the state basically assumes a monopoly not only over physical violence but over the meaning of violence as such – which is now defined as a violation of the meaning of religion.

It is precisely this *legal* monopoly that Deleuze and Guattari refer to when they remind us that the State-form "appear[ed] fully armed, a master stroke executed all at once ... the eternal model of everything the state wants to be and desires" (Deleuze & Guattari, 1988: 448). Or, to use Derrida's phrase for the legal monopolization of violence, the state exerts a kind of "juridico-symbolic" violence (Derrida, 1992: 37) – a violence embedded within the structures of language, logic, and law – that is present from the founding moment of the state and contributes to creating the very entity that it stands opposed to – specifically in this case religion.

The "juridico-symbolic" violence gives the impression of a mystical peaceful origin of state sovereignty even though it is founded on violence and its erasure. Such an impression is crucial for hiding the smooth functioning of the State-form, particularly its ability to foster belief in its creation myth and its objective framing of the meaning of violence *as*

---

[4] My understanding of *saeculum* follows Charles Taylor for whom this term refers to "the time of ordinary historical succession" and denotes a consciousness of being separated from the past, which is, of course, a Christian past (*A Secular Age*, 2007).

a violation of pacifist origin. It is this belief system, this "systemic violence" of conventional understanding (Žižek, 2008) and its "dogmatic image" (Deleuze, 1994) that is replicated endlessly by the State-form's de facto functionaries: policymakers, the media, and academia. And, as stated above, it is this conventional violence that has been deployed in modern narrative explanations of Sikh violence, most of which have been folded under the purview of historicism.[5]

---

[5] As Reinhart Kosselleck argues, the major problem with historicism is its claim to be a universal theory of time-consciousness, a claim that becomes hegemonic as it strives to legitimate itself as a science (of history). Closely scrutinized, however, it is effectively an ideology for controlling and governing time which it achieves by privileging a specific mode of "everyday" consciousness (Koselleck, 2002).

Henri Bergson goes much further than Koselleck by referring to this time-consciousness as "reflective consciousness" (or representation) which "results from an intrusion of an idea of space into the domain of consciousness," thereby reducing time to space, to a linear passage of present ("now") moments that are fixed as points in space. Bergson notes that "when we speak of time, more often than not we think of a homogenous milieu where the events or facts of consciousness line themselves up, juxtaposing themselves as if in space, and succeed in forming a distinct multiplicity" (Guerlac, 2006: 62). In other words, historicism is a mode of knowledge that represents events as purely external phenomena taking place in an empirical, material world to which "we" can all bear witness by recording, counting, and measuring events in relation to other events, thereby establishing objectivity for such knowledge. If we take violence as an example of such "events" then violence can only be narrated as if it were an external phenomenon; violence has to happen in the external world.

Thus, from the perspective of historicism, an event can only correspond to external, empirical, material states of affairs that express the event in its being empirically recorded. Once recorded it can be reproduced as an identity, but it can never be repeated differently. It remains locked in a past origin. This is why histories of Sikhism written by authors as seemingly different as Malcolm, McLeod (outsiders) and Khushwant Singh (insiders) all assume that violence is purely external and therefore empirically recordable; to narrate violence is to narrate an unfolding of events in which an originally pacifist (*religious*) movement suddenly begins to engage with the world, and because the world (as *saeculum*) is governed by the State-form, the movement deviates from its pacifist origin and

Yet, as we shall see in the sections that follow, this dogmatic or conventional image of violence is at odds with understandings of violence deriving from the Sikh Gurus' own writings as well as other primary sources. These sources present ways of thinking about violence that resist absorption into the totalizing knowledge system and orders of meaning generated especially by the modern State-form. There is something excessive in the nonoppositional concepts deriving from the Sikh sources – *nirguṇ-sarguṇ*, Guru, *nām*, *akāl*, Khālsā, *shahīd*, *mīrī-pīrī*, *sant-sipāhī*, *shabad-gurū*, etc. – that resists total capture and interiorization by the conceptual matrix of any State-form. This resistance to capture suggests that key Sikh concepts (noted earlier) and modes of narration based on them, cannot be completely reduced to the "dogmatic image" of violence. In this way, Sikh concepts not only contest the conventional notion of violence, but, through comparative analysis, also force us to acknowledge the multiple valences of the term violence both within the Western lexicon, and even more so, from within the lexicons of non-Western traditions such as *sikhī*.

One way to complicate the dogmatic understanding of violence is to lay bare a key assumption underpinning the epistemic totality of the modern knowledge system: the assumption that only Western concepts can be used

falls into violence. In short, historicist consciousness accords to itself the status of sole arbiter of reality, as the only way of thinking objectively about time and depicting the truth about violence.

However, even in the history of Western thought, historicism is but one of multiple modes of time-consciousness that are just as much *in-the-world* without reducing events to external, representable phenomena. Unlike historicism these alternative modes of time-consciousness tend not to reduce time to successive points in space. One such mode of time is *aion* (as opposed to *chronos*) which operates according to a "more interior relation between time and its outside." Ultimately, the difference between historicist and nonhistoricist modes of time-consciousness is that historicism is operated by a subjectivity that remains strictly homogenous, self-identical and brooks no internal multiplicity (an ego), whereas *aionic* time-consciousness is operated by a subjectivity that is internally heterogeneous. Precisely this internally pluralistic consciousness and mode of time-consciousness can be found in Sikh philosophy (*gurmat*) to which I devote more attention as this Element progresses.

as resources for contemporary thought, or, conversely, that non-Western concepts are unusable for contemporary thought because they are not properly philosophical but "religious" at best, which is the reason they are consigned to the domain of history, and, ultimately, not deemed worthy of being shared with contemporary humanity in the way that Western concepts are. To acknowledge the vitality of Sikh concepts in praxes of living, in cultural memory, and thinking is to acknowledge the "coexistence of epistemic and ontological pluriversality" (Mignolo & Walsh 2018: 227). In short, it is to acknowledge that Sikh concepts coined and deployed in the writings of the Sikh Gurus themselves (*gurmat*) produce their own epistemology and ontology that, in turn, provides a perspective on reality that Sikhs try to apply to their everyday lives.

Sections 2 and 3 of this Element provide a philosophical overview of the concept of violence implicit in the writings of the Sikh Gurus (*gurbāṇī*).[6] It also looks at the way in which this concept of violence has been put into play by the early Sikh community. In effect, Sections 2 and 3 outline something like a Sikh theory of religion that is simultaneously a theory of violence, allowing us to glimpse a sovereignty that escapes the totalizing grasp of the State-form. For lack of more suitable terminology, I refer to this excessive violence as *sovereign violence* – effectively, an internal violence that cannot be simplistically opposed to something called religion, or reduced to the material logic of cause and effect.

Narrating Violence Through Different Orders of Time: Kāl *and* Akāl

By looking more closely at the work of Sikh concepts, it is possible to think about violence in a more nuanced way than methodological historicism

---

[6] For a different approach see "A Socio-Theological Approach to Understanding Religious Violence" in which Jurgensmeyer and Sheik highlight the importance of studying "epistemic worldviews" that are basically structures of knowledge about "ultimate reality" namely the "study of the logic of God". For Sheik and Jurgensmeyer it is ultimately this God-logic that gives rise to "religious violence" (see *The Oxford Handbook of Religion and Violence* eds. Mark Jurgensmeyer, Margo Kitts, and Michael Jerryson, 2013, pp. 624–6).

typically allows. The point of working with Sikh concepts is not to oppose or displace the historical approach, but rather to recognize the existence of alternative temporalities that can function alongside linear history in ways that potentially enrich its explanatory powers. By acknowledging the simultaneous coexistence of different orders of time with equally valid claims to reality, history's powers of narration are expanded, making it possible to proceed simultaneously on two distinct levels, two different ways of thinking and narrating the event. On the one hand, there is history, whose main preoccupation is with public external time. The historical approach makes sense of events by providing explanations in terms of cause and effect, telling us how a certain event came about, what made it possible, how it unfolded and eventually dissipated over time (Patton, 2010: 95). On the other hand, there is an equally real order of time that unfolds internally, in a duration comprised not of external linear moments in succession, but of rhythms, immaterial transformations that take place within subjectivity, which is to say, in the flow of lived experience. This order of time, which expresses internal im/material intensities accompanying external material "facts," is the *event as such*.

The concept of sovereign violence as it emerges from Sikh textual sources provides a good example of how enunciations of the event of violence can participate in two contradictory, albeit overlapping, temporalities: *kāl* versus *akāl*. As noted above, there is phenomenal, external violence that takes place in ordinary everyday time (*kāl*) as part of the state of affairs of the public world governed by a statist logic of cause and effect. But there is also a rather different narrative sense, one where states of affairs and their recordings in historical time (*kāl*) are unable to fully circumscribe the event. There is an aspect of the event that is excessive, which lives on in the sense that it can be repeated differently by others, in different times and places. Every event contains a capacity to break with the past and give birth to new presents. In this sense, the event belongs to a completely different order of time – *akāl* – one that the State-form and its historicist frame can neither assimilate nor control.

Although it is a prevalent term in the writings of the Sikh Gurus, *akāl* is often interpreted as a negation of historical time (*kāl*), a move that leads to the translation of *akāl* as "immortal" or "eternity" signifying the foundational attribute of God's nature, namely, immutability. While not entirely wrong, this theologized translation suppresses a richer meaning of *akāl* that, rather than negating historical time, points to an ontologically deeper (in the sense of heterogenous) dimension of time that subsists simultaneously with *kāl* but cannot be accessed in the same way. This is because *akāl* as a concept does not refer to anything beyond the time of this world. It does not answer to a *theo*-logic and cannot therefore be relegated to "religious experience." Rather, *akāl* refers to the time of life *as it is becoming*, as it is being experienced, which demands an ontology more closely attuned to im/material transformations within subjectivity.

What is often forgotten in the modernist distinctions between *kāl* and *akāl* is that, although from an objective standpoint we treat them as modes of time, from a subjective standpoint they are modes of consciousness. Or better still, they are distinct but overlapping tendencies towards two different valences of consciousness: self-oriented individualism (which gives rises to *kāl* centrism) and ego-loss (*akāl*-centrism). Thus the difference between *kāl* and *akāl* is not their degree of reality – both are equally real even though they have different *modes* of existence – but the respective valence (gravitation towards ego versus gravitation away from ego; external/internal) that each represents. As I show in the next three sections of this Element, these distinct but overlapping tendencies are intimately connected to how violence is understood and categorized. Violence is not just publicly performed by agents on other agents or institutions. There is an equally real but different *sense* of violence as emerging primarily from internal transformations within the ego (a struggle of the self with itself) that cannot be measured in the same way we measure things in the world, but only through the *affect* that motivates psychological, social, and political change to happen.

Given this more expansive reading of temporality – one in which *kāl* and *akāl* are distinct but coexistent, co-implicated orders of time – it is possible to suggest that an actual event can give rise to *two entirely different senses* (Williams, 2008: 32–6).[7] One sense is aligned with an epistemology

---

[7] To entertain different senses of time is to look at violence "beyond" the cause/effect linear sense of time (*kāl*), which remains trapped in the perspective of states of affairs.

sanctioned by the State-form (*kāl*-centrism), whereas the other sense emerges from unlocking temporal frameworks associated with the concepts of *gurmat* (*akāl*-centric). It is important to note that the temporality of *akāl* is definitely not ahistorical, which would be a negation of historical time and the world we live in. Rather it corresponds to the temporality of life or lived experience that enjoys internal multiplicity and fosters the coexistence and co-implication of contradictory modes of time. Throughout this Element, *gurmat* functions methodologically to resist capture by the State-form's narrow mode of time (*kāl*). This can be seen in the consistent refusal of Sikh concepts to be subsumed under the pacifism–violence binary even when State-forms manage to successfully capture them, as is the case with modern Sikhism and its construction of Sikhs as a "martial race" (Section 3).

In effect, these opposed perspectives (statist versus *gurmat*) present a productive paradox. We have two *entirely real* but ultimately *incompatible* modes of time (*kāl* = ordinary linear time underpinning historicism, versus *akāl* = nonlinear time of life), which, in turn, translate into two different ways of conceptualizing violence in relation to an event. The simultaneous distinction and intersection between these two modes of time is, in turn, dependent on the non-oppositional ontology of *gurmat* that recognizes that what we call "reality" has a complexity that cannot be grasped within the mode of time in which our cognition normally operates, namely, the time of the present as constructed by the ego.

Reality, in its true sense, is irreducible to what exists before us. It can be spoken about in words, can be tagged with meaning, identified, and ultimately reduced to an object of knowledge. For this kind of reality, Nanak uses the qualifier *sarguṇ*. But there is an equally real mode of time in which things and events cannot be understood as objects of knowledge (they are not identifiable), and can only be grasped through creative means that allow access to a different mode of time (*akāl*) that is absolutely real but is not limited to the present. Nānak refers to this mode of reality as *nirguṇ*. For Nānak, *nirguṇ* and *sarguṇ* cannot be opposed. They are two parts of the same One. As we'll see in Sections 2 and 3, the intellectual work of keeping together the two sides of this reality that is *sarguṇ-nirguṇ* (One) at the same time, parallels the internal struggle within the human ego, to produce a mode of radical self-critique corresponding to what I have called sovereign violence.

Bicameral Approach to Interpreting Violence

Throughout this Element, I translate the nonoppositional logic of *kāl / akāl* described above into a formal method for presenting two different ways of interpreting violence. This can be seen in the organization of Sections 2, 3, and 4 into two subsections framed under *kāl* and *akāl*. In the *kāl* subsection, I briefly highlight actual instances of conventional external violence to Sikhs and by Sikhs as these events of violence have been recorded and discussed by historians. In terms of methodology, the *kāl/akāl* distinction is not entirely arbitrary. It resonates with a methodology developed by Deleuze and Guattari in texts such as *Logic of Sense* and *A Thousand Plateaus*,[8] in which these authors distinguish between two qualitatively different but parallel temporal registers they refer to as "States of Affairs" and "Lines of Flight," each of which respectively, and broadly, corresponds to the *kāl* and *akāl* frameworks described above. Thus "States of Affairs" refers to events from the standpoint of causal-linear, materialist history in which historians normally operate. "Lines of Flight," in contrast, refers to the im/material nature of events that cannot be captured by causal-linear time of the chronological present.

As a methodology this formal separation of temporal registers is necessary in order to respect the autonomies of historical and philosophical approaches that can have entirely different orientations towards the same phenomena. Accordingly, I begin Sections 2, 3, and 4 with a short section that provides a brief overview of the historical data on violence as "States of Affairs (*kāl*)" to indicate a minimally functional narrative limited to a few iconic instances of violence in Sikhism. The limited scope of this Element necessitates a highly selective approach for choosing such instances of violence. The aim is not to replicate the work of disciplinary historians. What I have in mind is far more modest. The "States of Affairs" section is

---

[8] For a helpful overview of Deleuze and Guattari's approach to history, see Craig Lundy, *History and Becoming*, Edinburgh: Edinburgh University Press, 2012.

therefore followed by the interpretive section "Lines of Flight" (*akāl*), which performs the philosophical work of enabling us to see violence as an incorporeal event, or what I refer to as internal or sovereign violence. The "Lines of Flight" (*akāl*) sections present a different way of *thinking about* violence based on the epistemic functionality of indigenous Sikh concepts.

By implementing this 'bicameral'[9] approach towards violence and time, my aim is to provide the beginnings of a methodology that juxtaposes two different senses of violence thereby complicating the conventional relationship between peace and violence. As hinted above, a bicameral approach is one that allows normally opposed understandings (*either/or*) to exist simultaneously (*both/and*). In this approach, normally opposed entities such as external violence and sovereign violence, history and event, *kāl* and *akāl* are more usefully read together rather than in opposition to one another. The success of the bicameral method hinges on being able to bring a limited philosophical analysis into dialogue with a minimal historical survey, with the aim of *holding together contradictory senses of violence and/or time* rather than succumbing to conventional dualisms such as historicism/tradition, or insider/outsider. Far from undermining the rich empirical work of historical scholarship, it operates intersectionally across and between disciplines rather than mining the depths of a single discipline, in the hope that scholars might reap the benefits accrued by diversifying the mode of critique, thus outweighing any perceived drawbacks of limited historical survey.

With this in mind, Section 2 revisits the writings of the Sikh Gurus (*gurbāṇī*) and the *purātan janāmsākhī* to extract a *nonviolent violence* associated with Nānak's inner struggle with ego, a conflict that leaves its imprint on Nānak's actions, speech, and thought and becomes the measure for transmitting authority. A more useful term that addresses the paradoxical nature of nonviolent violence is *sovereign violence*, a term I adopt throughout

---

[9] I have borrowed and adapted the term bicameral from William E. Connolly, who in turn follows Deleuze's *Logic of Sense*. The term bicameral normally refers to two equal but distinct legislative chambers of governance. It has also been in psychology to refer to two different but complementary functions of mind. In this Element, I adapt it to pluralize the logic in which events (of violence) are presented. See William E. Connolly (2005). *Pluralism*. Durham: Duke University Press, pp. 80–3.

the Element. The term sovereign violence helpfully points to the internal or psychic aspect of Guru Nānak's experience with *shabad-guru* or *anhad-shabad* – the incorporeal "Word that Kills."

"Internal" here means that the target of killing is not an external entity that can be objectively represented in historical time (*kāl*) but one's own ego. The annihilation of ego not only opens up the nonoppositional ontology of *akāl* but also brings the study of violence closer to a practical ethics, or more precisely, closer to theories of performativity that deal with the nature of the self as a doer rather than as a thing.[10] In this sense, the doing or acting that constitutes performativity, as I use this term in this Element, refers to the way in which one puts into practice what begins as an internal movement or struggle of the self *against itself*. This internal transforming of the self becomes the touchstone by which any external violence is measured. Thus the latter half of Section 2 describes how sovereign violence is *performatively enacted* by the succession of Sikh Gurus after Nānak, particularly in their dealings with the Mughal version of the State-form. Once again a paradox is shown to exist at the heart of any actual event or sequence of events.

Section 3 applies the performative aspect of sovereign violence developed earlier to the nonviolent resistances and martyrdom of the fifth and ninth Gurus at the hands of the Mughal state, demonstrating two different ways of envisaging the event. Either the Gurus were executed for transgressing Mughal law. Or they nonviolently resisted the state and in doing so performed a "sovereign violence," which impels the movement of history and causes the sense of this movement to be repeated by other actors. The

---

[10] Performativity has nothing to do with "theatricality" or "theater of violence," which Mark Jurgensmeyer has argued for in some of his earlier work (e.g. *Terror in the Mind of God*, California University Press: Berkeley, 1996). This particular notion of performativity presumes the meaning of violence to be primarily external or phenomenal. Jurgensmeyer uses performativity in the sense defined by J.L. Austin for whom the event or phenomenon is *for* an object-oriented consciousness. My use of performativity relies on a more expansive understanding of consciousness and follows a long line of critical theorists including Benjamin, Butler, Derrida, and many others. See also my discussion in Section 1 of this Element.

same paradox is encountered vis-à-vis the creation of a new order, the Khālsā, by the tenth Guru. Once again, my aim is not to provide an historiography of actual events, but to try and *extract the conceptual sense* of this event. By focusing on the concept of violence at work in the Khālsā's creation, it is possible to rethink old questions in a new light. Is this the creation of a new identity for the Sikhs (in the sense of a distinct physical body or military-religious order) or should the Khālsā be more usefully seen as a concept that can channel "sovereign violence" through its central motif of self-surrender or ego-loss? Is it a break with pacifism or a continuity of Nānak's central teaching? Answers to these questions depend on how we understand violence. Is the violence depicted in the creation of the Khālsā *kāl*-centric or *akāl*-centric, or both?

The last section of Section 3 asks what happens when the force of Nānak's philosophical concepts and/or the Khālsā as the embodiment of these concepts encounters modern colonial State-forms, as was the case with Maharaja Ranjit Singh's creation of a standing Khālsā army and the British imperial construction of Sikhs as a "martial race" and the reframing of Sikh tradition as an ethical monotheism. Do these cases where the *akāl*-centric sovereign violence of the Khālsā was harnessed in the service of Empire, thereby interdict Sikhs' self-understanding of internal violence and push it into a *kāl*-centric frame? In spite of this interdiction by the colonial state, modern Sikh existence continued to move between internal and external violence. For example, while Sikh soldiers and colonial elites buttressed British power in India, at the same time, other Sikhs (Akalis and Gadharites) tried to revive the spirit of sovereign violence in order to generate nonviolent insurrections against the British.

Section 4 shifts the focus back to the "spectacular" violence of terrorism and Sikh militancy in the late twentieth century by reinterpreting the violence associated with the "1984" episode indicated at the beginning of this section. Depending on whether we look at violence objectively or subjectively, the "1984" episode can be described either as the Indian Army's invasion of the Golden Temple to root out Sikh militants, or as a genuine act of antistate resistance by Sant Jarnail Singh Bhindranwale. My counterintuitive reinterpretation of the "1984" episode challenges the prevailing common sense about Sikh nationalism, identity politics, and the nature of Khālsā militancy. I argue that this "common sense" has obscured the "event nature" of 1984 by setting the entire narrative about Khālsā violence, identity, and Sikh nationalism within the *kāl*-centric image of time that idolizes "1984" in a form of memorialization grounded in homogenous, serial time of secular history. But what if this form of time is precisely what the state desires and has always desired, namely, to capture the Khālsā's sovereign violence and harness it to identity politics? What if *kāl*-centric identity politics is the ultimate form of violence against the *akāl*-centric sovereign violence taught and practiced by Guru Nānak?

2 Guru Nānak's Sovereign Violence

Guru Nānak was the founding figure in a lineage of ten spiritual masters, the Sikh Gurus, and the founder of what eventually evolved into the movement we know today as "Sikhism." The historical sources for Nānak's life are relatively limited and include the hagiographical literature known as *janām--sākhī* as well as the first *vār* of Bhai Gurdās, an important Sikh exegete who lived a century or so after Nānak. Nevertheless, historians have managed to construct a fairly reliable life narrative by sifting legend from probable fact (McLeod, 1968; Grewal, 1969). One result of this sifting has been the creation of an image of Guru Nānak not only as a peaceful saintly figure uninvolved in politics, averse to physical violence or confrontation, but also (because Nānak is widely accepted as the authoritative figure in all of Sikhism) as the pacifist exemplar in relation to all later developments involving violent interactions with the state or other agents. This clichéd image has been routinely replicated in academia, media, and by state agencies.

However, this image is, at best, only partially correct. At worst it is misleading, because what's often forgotten about this narrative-image is its reliance on a specific theology that has been imputed to Nānak's teachings, and from here to the whole of Sikhism. I begin the "States of Affairs (*kāl*)" section by highlighting, first, some plausible historical facts about Guru Nānak's life, second, a short overview of the theology that underpins the dominant narrative of Nānak as a strictly "religious" figure uninvolved in violence. The importance of this theology is its dependence on a peculiarly modern and state-centric notion of sui generis violence. This is followed in the "Lines of Flight (*akāl*)" section with a more complex interpretation of violence that emerges from Nānak's own compositions. What we see in these writings is a *nonviolent violence* associated with Nānak's inner struggle with ego. This is an internal or intrapsychic struggle resulting from Guru Nānak's experience with *shabad-guru* or *anhad-shabad* – the incorporeal "Word that Kills". "Internal" here means that the target of violence is not an external entity that can be objectively represented in historical time (*kāl*) but one's own ego. The annihilation of ego not only opens up the nonoppositional ontology of *akāl* but also sets the funda-mental ethical tone for what violence is and can be. As I explain in the "Lines of Flight (*akāl*)" section, not only does the internal violence of this psychic struggle leave its imprint on Nānak's actions, speech, and thought, it also becomes the measure for transmitting authority to his successors. A more useful term that addresses the paradoxical nature of nonviolent violence is *sovereign violence*, which is henceforth adopted throughout this Element.

States of Affairs-1 (kāl)

Guru Nānak was born in 1469 (CE hereafter) in Talwandi, a village forty miles from Lahore. He married and had two sons. Nānak received a formal education in Sanskrit, Arabic, and Persian, giving him access to employment with the elite classes of Punjabi society. However, he was less concerned with settling into a comfortable profession, as his parents had hoped, than with a spiritually motivated concern to uplift downtrodden societies and bridge cultural differences between Hindus and Muslims. The first sign of such socio-spiritual concerns at the early age of twelve was his outright rejection of a prime marker of orthodox Hindu identity, namely, the *janaeu* or sacred thread worn by twice-born or initiated Hindus. In some sense, this can be seen as Nānak's first act of revolt, an uncompromising resistance against one of the foundational pillars of Vedic orthodoxy, and directed at the fundamental inequality of the Hindu society he had been born into (Singh & Ashok, 1962/1969; Singh, 1996: 24–37).

After this event, Nānak became increasingly indifferent to worldly pursuits and preferred to seek out the company of holy men and ascetics. During his adolescent years, periodic cycles of melancholy and ecstatic bliss began to manifest themselves in Nānak's personality. At around the age of nineteen Nānak left his ancestral village and found work as an accountant at Sultanpur. As his life settled into a more regulated pattern, the earlier cycles of melancholia were channeled into more productive contemplative practice. During the day Nānak would settle the village accounts, but he spent much of the night engrossed in meditative practices such as *nām simaran* (repetition of the "Name") and *kīrtan* or devotional singing. Together with his close associate, a Muslim bard named Mardana, Nānak organized regular nightly *kīrtan* sessions, after which he went to bathe in a nearby river before daybreak (Singh & Ashok, 1962/1969).

Sometime in 1499, after one of these sessions, Nānak is reported to have undergone a definitive mystical experience in which he received a calling to teach people a path of devotion to the divine Name. This experiential event that took place in Sultanpur is generally recognized as the culminating experience in Nānak's search for his true vocation, marking the achievement of spiritual perfection. Soon after this, the fully enlightened master, now recognized as a Guru in his own right, set out to teach his message to the rest of the world. After twelve years of extensive travel and teaching Guru Nānak founded a settlement at Kartarpur where he led a community of disciples, instructing them in spiritual practice and study making *nām simaran* and *kīrtan* regular features of devotion, but at the same time insisting that his disciples remain fully involved in worldly affairs by undertaking practical labor in the midst of a regular family life. By the time of his death in 1539 Nānak left behind a young but functioning community with a distinctive ethos and forms of practice. More importantly, he appointed a successor fully authorized to continue the development of the early Sikh community. Thus began a politico-spiritual lineage lasting two centuries, the so-called "house of Nānak," in which each successor inherited the guruship (*gurgaddī*) and the authority of the name "Nānak" (Singh & Ashok, 1962/1969).

But the key legacy that Nānak left to his successor and to the fledgling community was a body of authoritative compositions containing the crux of his teachings and ideas. The specific nature of this teaching provided continuity and focus for his successor Gurus and the growing community particularly in the face of violence perpetrated by powerful state actors and authorities against later Sikh Gurus. For this reason alone it is important to take a closer look at the nature of Guru Nānak's teaching because the way this teaching is interpreted and defined crucially affects our understanding of the relationship between religion and violence in its application in scholarly and media narratives about the evolution of Sikhism.

For example, since the colonial era, scholars have tried to pin down the exact nature of Guru Nānak's teaching by defining Sikhism's core religiosity as *nirguṇa bhaktī*. In the late nineteenth century, historians of religion reinterpreted indigenous understandings of devotional practice in India by arguing that it could be divided into two types: *saguṇa bhaktī* and *nirguṇa bhaktī*, which refer to two very different concepts of the divine. *Saguṇa bhaktī* or devotion to a god who has attributes, qualities or form, refers to a god that exists. This was attributed to the path of Hindu devotion to a personal god, for example, Vishnu, a god who exists, has tangible form, and could be represented through images, icons, and idols. According to the theological interpretation of Western historians of religion, *saguṇa bhaktī* gave rise to an exterior piety that produced conflicting truth-claims and therefore had the potential to catalyze communal violence. By contrast, *nirguṇa bhaktī* is devotion to a god without attributes, qualities, or form, and insofar, an ineffable god who does not interfere in the temporal world of states and affairs. A relatively recent version of this thesis reappeared in the work of leading historians of South Asian religion, their argument being that the path of *nirguṇa bhaktī*, in which worship of idols and images representing the divine are forbidden, was also followed by the sants or *bhagats* and by Guru Nānak.[11] Since the focus of devotion is a formless,

---

[11] This interpretation of the core of sant and Sikh religiosity has been propagated notably by W. H McLeod in some key works. See for example W. H. McLeod and Karine Schomer, *The Sants: A Study of a Devotional Tradition of North India*, New Delhi: Motilal Banarsidas, 1987. As McLeod and Schomer both acknowledge (p. 3) the *nirguṇa bhaktī* thesis "is relatively new" and can probably be traced to the works of North Indian colonial elites such as Pitambar

ineffable God, the nature of its core religiosity is strictly *interiorized*. It follows that because such interiorized piety is amenable to *privatization*, it is far less likely to produce conflicting truth claims about the nature of God that in turn might lead to communal violence.

There are several obvious problems with this model. First, the idea of an opposition between *saguṇa* and *nirguṇa bhaktī* was itself an Orientalist construct modelled on a secularized Christian theology (King, 1999). It does not correspond to the actual nature of piety in Hindu and Sikh devotion. Neither the *bhagats* nor Guru Nānak ever used the terms *saguṇa* or *nirguṇa bhaktī* to name their concept of God or the nature of their religiosity. Second, since the late nineteenth century, Orientalists and Christian missionaries tried to fit nonoppositional Indic concepts into a Christian theological framework, which was the only conceptual framework available to them. Devotion was understood in the Christian sense in terms of the central definition of God's nature: that God exists, and cannot *not* exist. Basically Indic concepts were reframed according to a Western concept of religion which defined "proper religion" as "essentially interior" and amenable to privatization. This interiorized concept of Indian religion, for which *nirguṇ bhaktī* is the exemplary form of a peaceful Indian mysticism grounded in "personal experiences" and "individual conscience", was a central tool in the colonial ordering of India by removing Indian thought and cultural practice from the exercise of worldly, public power (Cavanaugh, 2008: 91). As William Cavanaugh and Peter Van de Veer have argued in different contexts, this was part of a broader strategy that the British

---

D. Barthwal's *The Nirguṇa School of Hindi Poetry* (1936) and Parashuram Chaturvedi's 1952 study *Uttari Bharat ki sant-paramparā* (*The Sant Tradition of North India*). Moreover, even a cursory study of these two works shows the extent to which Barthwal and Chaturvedi had internalized imperialist constructions of North Indian religions by Orientalists writing in the late nineteenth and early twentieth century. In the writings of these Orientalists, the *nirguṇa bhaktī* thesis is modelled on a secularized Christian theology that has been uncritically replicated by many scholars. A relatively recent example is Doris Jakobsch's *Sikhism*, University Press, 2012, pp 18–19.

imperial state used to privatize concepts of religion and religiosity so that it could claim a monopoly on the use of violence in law making and thereby influence public allegiance.

This entire model for perceiving religion and violence is rendered even more problematic when we look closely at Guru Nānak's own concepts which renders all manner of binary oppositions – *nirguṇa/saguṇa bhaktī*, rational/nonrational, public/private, interior religion/exterior religion, violence/pacifism – meaningless. In the "Lines of Flight" section, I show how some of Guru Nānak's key concepts can be used to track a more complex understanding of violence that can be translated into practice.

Lines of Flight 1 (akāl)

Tracking a Concept of Violence in Guru Nānak's Philosophy

A succinct expression of Nānak's teaching is encapsulated by the syllable *ik oankār*, which appears at the very beginning of Nānak's most authoritative hymn, the *Japjī*, and is repeated over and again in the central Sikh scripture or Guru Granth Sahib. In most modern translations and exegeses, this syllable has by and large been rendered in accordance with the rationalized idiom of monotheism as "One God Exists" or "There is One God."[12] A more suitable translation might be: "One (*ik*), whose expression (*oan*) unfolds in all beings in the same way (*kār*)."

According to Guru Nānak, this One is neither thing nor predicate. 'One' signifies a state of existence in the world, both psychological and physical. Insofar as it is a state, this One is qualitative, sovereign and therefore absolute. This state of absolute Oneness can only be realized through experience[13] and expressed only through paradox. Thus we can speak of this One as personal, as a feeling of an infinitely close presence, and we can give this infinitely close presence a variety of names such as Madho, Hari,

---

[12] Variations of this can be found in almost all translations of *ik oankār*, which tend to follow the pattern established by modernist-reformist exegeses.

[13] This is evident from the opening lines of the *Japjī*'s *mul mantar* or creedal statement.

Ram, suggesting the experience is of a personal God who takes manifold forms (*sarguṇ*). But, at the same time, the experience cannot be grasped by our mind for this very same One is also impersonal and formless (*nirguṇ*) experienced as continually slipping away. It becomes absent in the very moment that we say something positive about it, such as a name or quality, for instance. So the One, according to Nānak, is both absent and present at the same time.

But the problem, as Nānak sees it, is that our attempts to experience this state constantly fail because we filter through the human ego what should be experienced directly. Instead of experiencing the One directly, the ego generates a false perception of reality, splitting it into a duality which masquerades as an illusory oneness generated through the desire for self-gratification.[14] According to Nānak, once this dualism sets in, it begins to color the way that individuals and societies relate to the One. Thus different people speak of the One, but they fail to realize that the One remains One (*ēk*) even though its projected forms are Many (*anēk*). Some social groups think that the Many must be subordinate to the One, which is thereby conceived as a transcendent entity, while others think and practice the exact opposite.

Guru Nānak noticed this dualism at work in the cultural and religious divide between Muslims and Hindus. For example, both Hindus and Muslims say that God is One but they conceptualized this Oneness in opposing ways. While Hindus say that God is infinitely near to us, infinitely present in all things, and try to express this proximity through the tangible presence of images and idols, Muslims regard this One as transcendent, infinitely beyond us. But for Nānak, this opposition prevented either social group from experiencing the One. This is why Nānak's own experience was initially articulated as: "There is no Hindu, there is no Muslim" – implying that both groups missed the experience that must include the other. As such they stopped being Hindu and Muslim. Instead, both traditions began to emphasize the social projections of the divine, and through these social projections began pitting themselves against one another.

---

[14] See stanza 1 of the *Japjī*.

For Nānak, external social projections of an entity called 'God' simply reflected the internal anxiety of a deluded ego, thereby reducing "God" to the status of a thing among all other existing things, making it a plaything for politicians. Instead he argued that devotees should focus attention on the faculty that does the projecting, namely, ego, mind, or self. It is the ego's apparatus that at the same time *prevents* the experience and yet is the very *means* of that experience. To make this clearer, Nānak suggests a more workable formula by asking the devotee to keep in mind that God (or the experience of the One) and ego cannot be in the same place at the same time. Listen to what both Nānak and Kabir say on this issue:

> Nānak
> *When I act in ego, You're not present.*
> > *When you're present, ego is absent.*
> *O Nānak repeat these words: "He is me, I'm him"*
> > *In this Oneness the three modes of time are merged.*

> Kabir:
> *When I am, Hari is not.*
> > *Now Hari is, and I am no more.*
> *By saying "You, You" I have become You*
> > *"I am" is in me no longer.*

Guru Nānak refers to individuals who limit their understanding of "God" to social projection and its inherently dualistic mode of perception as *manmukh* – indicating an ego-centered and therefore unfree or ignorant state of mind/existence. As Nānak states in the opening stanzas of *Japjī*, the One cannot be experienced through rituals or conceptual abstraction, through mere silencing of the mind or by constantly feeding ones cravings.[15] The ego works by routing our experience of the absolute One through all manner of repetition: concepts, rituals, or austerities. Consequently, the One fails to be experienced as such; the

[15] Stanza 1, *Japjī*.

nearest we get is to represent it as an object or an idol to constantly gratify the ego's desire for permanence.

Violating Ego

This of course begs the question: If ego is the problem, what then is the remedy? To get rid of ego completely? This would surely entail some form of extreme austerity or social renunciation which Nānak emphatically rejected. How then to attain realization of the desired state of Oneness?[16]

Guru Nānak's answer is simple but somewhat unconventional. Rather than getting rid of the ego altogether, he instructs the devotee to battle the ego's sense of self-attachment, and thereby restructure the ego altogether. One has to become a kind of spiritual warrior capable of acknowledging that our own ego prevents us from undergoing the experience, but at the same time, realize that there is "something" within it that provides a remedy to the problem and enables us to undergo the experience.[17]

This "something" is an imperative (*hukam*), a fundamental law that constitutes the very order of nature itself and sustains the alignment and functioning of all existence. All existence is aligned with and according to *hukam*. Everything, that is, except ego or *haumai* (lit. "I-am-ness" to use Nānak's own term). Left to its own devices, ego or *haumai* violates *hukam* by setting itself up as an alternate law in opposition to *hukam* through its ability to propagate itself as an autonomous individuating entity (an "I am"). It would seem, therefore, that in order to address the problem of failing experience, the solution is to realign the ego with *hukam*. The problem is this: How is one to recognize *hukam*, if ego's very function is to weave around itself an illusion of its own autonomy, which ultimately works to sever our access to or recognition of *hukam*?

Again, Nānak's answer is deceptively simple. If ego violates *hukam*, and if ego won't listen because of its delusions of autonomy, then it is

---

[16] Stanza 2, *Japjī* : *kiv sachiarā hoiai, kiv kurai tutai paal?*

[17] This dual nature of ego is also outlined in hymn *Āsā dī Vār*, M2, 7.2, SGGS, p. 466.

necessary to commit a nonviolent violence against ego, a kind of self-violation that stops short of annihilating ego. In stanza 2 of *Japjī*, Nānak states that "in order to recognize *hukam* and for it to take effect, let the ego not say 'I am myself' (*haumai*)." So the imperative (*hukam*) is "Let ego not say I am myself" (*tā haumai kahai nā koi*). In simple, although paradoxical, terms, what this implies is that the individual should speak/act/think in such a way that one resists ego-centrism (*haumai*) even as ego continues to be formed. In other words, the ego must learn to silence itself but without ceasing to exist. For Nānak, this silencing is not to be understood literally. It refers instead to an internal struggle resulting in a self-enforced withdrawal of ego at the very moment that the self names itself as "I" and thus starts to become an origin or absolute center in relation to all other existing things.

The Word that Kills: Sword of the Spiritual Warrior (*gurmukh*)

This violent internal struggle of the self with itself, or "self-enforced withdrawal," has a peculiarity that needs to be clarified. First, if the phrase itself sounds violent that is precisely what it is. Like other spiritual masters, Nānak refers to it as an "annihilation" of ego, an annihilation that the ego must carry out on itself and still manage to survive. Yet such annihilation is neither literal, nor final. Rather its ultimate purpose is to annihilate the "I saying" function of the self – its proclivity for self-attachment – and replace it with a psychic formation whose characteristic speech is "I am not" – an ultimate form of humility that obeys the fundamental imperative (*hukam*) by sacrificing that entity which the ordinary person regards as his or her ownmost: one's ego.

Second, self-enforced withdrawal (or self-detachment) could be mis-conceived as being instigated by the ego's own effort, something like a self-power. However, precisely the opposite is the case. For Nānak, the power to enact such annihilation of the ego comes from a nonhuman principle, the *satguru* (lit. true guru) which is not a person but a nonhuman principle, specifically the Word or *shabad*. Indeed, in one particular dialogue with a group of spiritual adepts known as the Siddhas, Nānak emphatically expressed that his own guru or master from whom he attained perfection is *shabad* (the Word):

The Word is my Guru, the consciousness attuned to it, its disciple
shabad guru surat dhun chela[18]

It is the Word (*shabad*) that annihilates the self and at the same time gives rise to a transformed individual (the *gurmukh*) with a radically different psychic formation. Throughout his writings Nānak makes constant reference to "dying to the Word." The Word is the sword that annihilates the ego and gives birth to the unspoken Word (*anhad shabad*), which corresponds to the transformed speech/thought/actions of the *gurmukh*.

Two things need to be underscored here about the nature of this internal violence, which can more usefully be termed "sovereign violence." First, such violence is sovereign because it depends on no one or no thing other than itself. One way of envisaging this fundamental nondependence is to think of the psychic formation *gurmukh* as constantly self-differing, thereby resisting any desire to concentrate sovereignty within itself. In other words, sovereign violence is fundamentally non-violent because it emanates from the activity of self-differentiation. By harnessing its own internal difference the *gurmukh* can assemble force in alternative ways, giving rise to new forms of social relation other than those specified by any State-form.

Second, the activity that comprises sovereign violence consists in self-differentiation – the capacity and will to differentiate oneself internally. This is an activity that erases ego but without annihilating it. As such it is at the heart of Nānak's mystical experience such as the one he is said to have experienced at Sultanpur – one he exhorts others to emulate and attain in their own ways. Self-differentiation is a fundamental violence best described as a violence directed towards the ego's desire to be sovereign; it is an absolutely interior violence enacted on one's own self, which then becomes the measure by which all external or physical violence between people must be understood:

> *Those who battle with their own mind are true heroes*
> *Curbing the mind, by the Guru's grace, they conquer the world.*

[18] *GGS*, Siddh Gosht, pp. 938–46, v. 44.

> *Ignorant ones try to kill their minds through asceticism, but fail to kill*
> *   its cravings*
> *Nānak: the mind is overcome only by reflecting on the Word*
>
> *All seek to still the mind but fail.*
> *Only through the* satguru *can the mind overcome the mind.*[19]

Thirdly, this capacity for sovereign violence is directly linked to Nānak's claim to authority. It is what makes him Guru or master of a new teaching and a new community. Yet such authority only comes, paradoxically, from Nānak's renunciation of his own ego-speech, his absolute submission to the principle of *hukam* and the figure of the *satguru* – which opens the portals of a new mode of speech/action/thought embodied by the figure of *gurmukh*. For Nānak, this subjection of one's will to ultimate sacrifice – to sacrifice one's own ego and enact self-transformation (thereby becoming a *gurmukh*) – was not just an ideal but needed to become a spiritual technique that he *performatively* illustrated in several different ways, both during his lifetime and after his death. Guru Nānak used self-sacrifice as a touchstone not only to appoint and pass on his authority to a new successor (who in effect becomes the new "Nānak") but also, in his encounters with contemporary rulers such as the first Mughal emperor Babur. He used it to challenge the moral authority of kings and administrators who deployed physical violence to stake their claim to power and dominion over others. Let us look at each of these performances of self-sacrifice or sovereign violence in turn.

Performing Sovereign Violence 1: Early Encounters with the Mughal State

In many ways, the nature of Guru Nānak's encounter with the first Mughal emperor Babur defined the tenor of future relationships between the respective successors of Nānak and Babur and whether that relationship was dominated by peace or conflict, violence or nonviolence. According to Pashaura Singh, Guru Nānak's compositions in a section of the Guru Granth Sahib (Sikh scripture) collectively referred to as

---

[19] GGS, p. 1089.

Bābur-vāṇī (Utterances Concerning Babur) provide "an eyewitness account of Babur's invasion of India" as well as a "powerful critique of both the invaders and rulers" thereby focusing attention on the indiscriminate violence against Hindu and Muslim alike that took place under Babur's watch (Singh, 2017: 173–90). Nānak's encounter with Babur probably took place around the time that Babur's armies were busy making a series of incursions into Northern India and Nānak himself was returning from tours to the Middle East. Guru Nānak may have witnessed at least one such incursion.[20]

The *janamsākhī* literature and the *vārs* of Bhai Gurdās build a more embellished account based on the *Bābur-vāṇī* verses and weave a narrative in which Guru Nānak stayed at Sayyidpur with his disciple Bhai Lalo on his return from Medina and Baghdad.[21] According to this narrative, Lalo complained about the mistreatment of ordinary people by the ruling Lodi dynasty. In response to Lalo, Nānak uttered a prophetic warning that the dominion of the Lodi's would soon be over as Babur had already departed from Kabul and embarked on a conquest of India. However, the conquest would not end with the destruction of the Lodi dynasty but would bring ruin and destruction across Punjab. Entire populations in towns like Sayyidpur would become "cities of corpses" as Babur's armies massacred and plundered their way to the capital Delhi. In fact, shortly after his visit to Lalo, Guru Nānak himself, along with his companion Mardana, was captured and imprisoned by the invading army and forced into slave labor alongside hundreds of displaced women who overnight had become the spoils of war. Pained by the plight of these women, Nānak fell into a trance

---

[20] Pashaura Singh's article "Speaking Truth to Power: Exploring Guru Nānak's Babur-vani in Light of the Baburnama," provides a comprehensive discussion of the literature pertaining to Guru Nānak's encounter with Babur. *Religions*, 2020, 11, p. 1–19. An earlier discussion of these issues can be found in Surjit Singh Gandhi. *History of the Sikh Gurus*. New Delhi: Gurdās Kapur and Sons, 1978: 38–49

[21] The fact that "Lalo" is directly mentioned in the Guru Granth Sahib by Guru Nānak (Rag Tilang p. 722) strongly suggests that the *janamsākhī* narrative is based on events that actually happened.

state and expressed his anguish through a powerful indictment that attracted the attention of the Mughal officers:

Babur ruled over Khurasan and now terrorizes Hindustan.

Nānak's words were conveyed to Babur, who went to the prison to meet the Guru. Thus, according to *janāmsakhi* accounts and Bhai Gurdās' *vārs*, began a series of encounters between the house of Nānak (a spiritual master) and the house of Babur (a warlord, soon to become emperor). The encounter began with the Guru's nonviolent remonstration against the warlord's excessive and unjust use of force against innocent civilians. Accepting these failings, the warlord ordered prisoners to be released, but, in turn, begged the Guru to bless his future empire. Nānak replied that Babur's empire would remain for some time, but, as emperor, he should be just and merciful in his judgments and treatment of his subjects, respect religious traditions other than his own, and uphold truthful practice. In their final exchange, Babur pressed the Guru to embrace Islam and the Prophet Muhammad to help him achieve his spiritual goals and align with the ruling faith. To this, Guru Nānak replied in outspoken terms that there are "thousands of prophets like Muhammad sent into this world time and again, but only one Creator."

Hukam versus *Hukūmat*

For the writers of the *janāmsakhis*, this early encounter set the future terms of engagement between the house of Nānak and the house of Babur. Both men claimed authority, but their power came from two completely different sources. Babur's exercised state power or *hukūmat* backed by the over-whelming physical violence of his armies, with the legal and moral backing of the state religion – Islam. By contrast, Guru Nānak exercised power through an interior violence derived not from *hukūmat* (state power) but from a submission to *hukam* – an interior violence in which one dies to the self – a violence that is absolutely excessive (in the sense that *hukam* infinitely exceeds *hukūmat*) and cannot be captured or contained by state power. Unlike Babur's authority, Nānak's authority derived from a realized truth: that no worldly power can force the self to violate its own self-sacrificial nature, except by conferring martyrdom on it. For Guru Nānak, the true state is marked by a realization of Oneness within, which must be a prerequisite for any external state.

Performing Sovereign Violence 2: Transmission of Guruship

This essential distinction between interior and exterior violence, the excessive violence of self-sacrifice, and the violence of self-preservation, would be performatively demonstrated through the mechanism whereby authority was transmitted from Nānak to his successors. Arguably the most important institution inaugurated by Guru Nānak was the institution of guruship, insofar as it provided a mechanism for consolidating and continuing his work after his death. The institution of guruship entailed much more than simply nominating a successor. It was intrinsically connected to the question of Nānak's authority as Guru, and thus to the sovereignty of the teaching and practice that he had created. Nānak had experienced the sublime truth of existence at the most profound level, which he was convinced could change the nature of the self and society. Yet the complexities of the social, political, and cultural milieu in which he lived prevented him from completing his task before the end of his life. Clearly, it was necessary to find some person who could continue Nānak's work in accordance with the founder's own intentions. But what was to be the touchstone for choosing a new successor? If the touchstone were proximity to the master himself, then an obvious choice might have been Guru Nānak's own family, perhaps one of his own two sons. However, both sons "proved intractable and disobedient," and failed a number of tests that were designed by the Guru to probe his disciples' inner qualities.[22]

The person eventually chosen to succeed him was Bhai Lehna whose service, devotion, and humility were recognized by Guru Nānak and his inner circle who regarded Lehna as an exemplary and inspirational figure. The various tests to which Lehna was put displayed his proximity to the cardinal virtues that Nānak desired in his successor: humility, complete devotion, respect for the householder's life, but, perhaps most importantly, a poetic consciousness that drew from the same wellspring of spiritual experience as

---

[22] Bhaī Gurdās, *Vāran* – Satta and Balwand, *Tikkī di Vār* (Coronation Ode), *Paurī* 2–3

Nānak. Central to this poetic sensibility was the concept of *shabad-guru*: the idea that the ultimate Guru (or *satguru*) is the *shabad* (Word), rather than a human guru. And this nonhuman principle can only be realized by "dying to the Word," by sacrificing ego on the sword of the Word. In order to succeed Nānak as the new Guru, Lehna would have had to demonstrate this principle to his mentor. It is this qualitative proximity that the *janāmsakhis* speak of as the passing of light from one body to another. Accordingly, to indicate the succession of guruship, in the last months of his life Guru Nānak renamed Lehna as Angad (lit. part of my own body). Prostrating himself before his successor, Nānak proclaimed to the Kartarpur community that Angad would be their new Guru, the new "Nānak" (Gandhi, 1978: 168–72).

This act of prostration of the master before his disciple was a profoundly important event in the formation of the early Sikh community and carried strong theological and social meaning that sent out several important signals (see Figure 1). First, that Nānak intended for his work to be continued. Second, that it was possible for any of his Sikhs to achieve the perfected state of *gurmukh* within one's lifetime, and that the positions of Guru and Sikh were interchangeable – they were not divinely ordained. In other words, there was, potentially at least, no difference, spiritually, poetically, philosophically, between the founder and his successor(s), between master and disciple.

But, in order for the transmission of authority between master and disciple to take effect, it was necessary for the disciple's act of surrender / devotion/ self-sacrifice to be equaled or surpassed by the master who, by surrendering to his disciple, committed an act of ultimate sacrifice in the form of *self-violation*, a violence to the perceived image of him as divine. In order to put the succession into motion Nānak had to *publicly enact self-loss*, a death of the self premised conceptually on the principle of *shabad-guru*. It is this *free and willing exchange of ego-loss* (one by the Sikh, the other by the Guru) that not only set in motion the historical transmission of guruship, but provided doctrinal focus and continuity of practice for the early Sikh community as it would evolve over the next two centuries. Indeed, this paradoxical doctrine of ego-loss as dying to the Word encapsulated the sovereign principle of Guru Nānak's teaching (*gurmat*). If the sovereignty of this teaching is defined by a violence directed towards the desire to concentrate sovereignty in one's own self, then sovereign violence resides at the core of Guru Nānak's teaching.

Figure 1 Performing sovereign violence – the master renounces personal sovereignty by surrendering to his disciple who becomes the new Guru. [Credit: http://www.namdhari-world.com/. Artist unknown.]

3 Martyrdom, Militancy, and the Khālsā

States of Affairs 2 (kāl)

After the death of Guru Nānak in 1539, the growing Sikh community was consolidated under the leadership of the second, third, and fourth gurus (Angad, Amardas, and Ramdas). This early phase of expansion coincided with the reign of Babur's grandson, the Emperor Akbar, who cultivated good relations with non-Muslim subjects. Due partly to minimal interference from the Mughal state during this period, the fifth Guru, Arjan was able to lead the Sikh community to a new level of economic prosperity and socio-religious development. He established the city of Amritsar as a central place of pilgrimage and commerce and compiled a new scripture (the Adi Granth).

However, the growing strength of the Sikh community and Guru Arjan's personal influence in the region, which was strategically situated on the main route between the most important sites of the Mughal empire, was gained at the risk of becoming involved in imperial affairs (Shackle & Mandair, 2005: xv). Moreover, there was growing opposition from rival claimants to Guru Arjan's authority and stewardship of Guru Nānak's teaching which accorded sovereign authority to a nonpersonal principle (*shabad-guru*) in place of a personal living guru. Acutely aware of these internal animosities, Arjan not only foresaw a politics of succession unfolding in both the early Sikh community and the young Mughal dynasty, but also began to think about defensive measures in preparation for a time when the Mughal state would reverse its tolerant policy towards Sikhs and other non-Muslims.[23]

The reversal in state policy came into effect almost immediately after Akbar's death prompting the expected wars of succession. The new emperor Jahangir drew powerful support from Sunni orthodox circles opposed to Akbar's liberal policy towards non-Muslims. Even prior to his

---

[23] One of the most important witnesses to the politics of the day as it affected the early Sikh community was Bhaī Gurdās Bhalla, who composed an important body of literature (*Varān*, ed. Giani Hazara Singh, Amritsar: Khālsā Samachar, 1962). As well as being related to the Gurus, Bhaī Gurdās' life overlapped with the reign of Guru Amar Das and Ramdas and he was closely connected to Guru Arjan, and Guru Hargobind. He witnessed the transition from peaceful rule of Akbar to the more hostile reign of Jahangir and Shah Jahan. For biographical details of Bhaī Gurdās, see Rattan Singh Jaggi, *Bhaī Gurdās: Jivan te Rachna*, Patiala: Punjabi University, 1974. He writes in detail about the role of those like Prithi Chand (whom he refers to as *miṇas*, in bringing about circumstances leading to the death of Guru Arjan and hardships faced by Guru Hargobind). See especially Bhaī Gurdās, *Var* 26, and 36.

accession, entries in his personal diary suggest that Jahangir was irritated by Guru Arjan's rising popularity with Muslims and Hindus in the region:

> In Goindval, which is on the river Beas, there was a Hindu named Arjun, who pretended to be a saint, whose manners and ways bewitched the minds of simple-minded Hindus, and even ignorant Muslims, such that these followers regarded him as holy. They called him "Guru," and from all sides foolish people crowded to express their faith in him. For three or four generations [of Nānak's successors] this false traffic continued. Many times it occurred to me either to put an end to this vain affair or to bring him into the fold of Islam (Singh, 1949: 20–22).

The tipping point for Jahangir came when his main rival to the Mughal throne, his eldest son Khusrau Mirza, instigated a rebellion that backfired. While fleeing Jahangir's army, Khusrau took temporary refuge at Goindval close to where Guru Arjan was staying. The emperor's spies reported the meeting as a seditious political alignment between Arjan and Khusrau. Whatever the nature of the Guru's meeting with Khusrau, it gave Jahangir the pretext to take punitive action against Arjan. Within a month, Guru Arjan was summoned to Lahore to stand trial on what appeared to be politically motivated charges. In addition to treason, the Guru was accused of (i) encouraging his devotees to refer to him as "the true King" (*sacha padshah*); (ii) increasing his following to make war on the state; (iii) building an autonomous power base. What these charges effectively boiled down to was a perceived threat to the sovereignty of the Mughal state. According to Jahangir's diary, the Guru was ordered to pay a fine and admit the charges of treason, or convert to Islam.[24] The Guru's

---

[24] See Pashaura Singh, *Life and Work of Guru Arjan*, New Delhi: Oxford University Press, 2010; Louis Fenech, *The Darbar of the Sikh Gurus*, New Delhi: Oxford University Press, 2008; J. S. Grewal, *Sikh Ideology, Polity and Social Order*, New Delhi: Manohar 1996.

refusal on both accounts led to his being sentenced to death by extreme torture in April 1606:

> At length, when Khusrau passed by there, this inconsequential little fellow [Arjan] proposed to wait on him. Khusrau halted at the place where he was and paid homage to him. He behaved to Khusrau in a special way and marked his forehead with saffron, which the Hindus consider propitious ... When I learned of this, I knew his folly and ordered him to be produced, his dwelling-places seized and his children handed over to Murtaza Khan ... Having confiscated his property I commanded that he be put to death.
>
> (Thackston, 1999: 59)

As Pashaura Singh notes, the execution of Guru Arjan was a particularly traumatic event for the early Sikh community from whose point of view his death was a "martyrdom [and] became the decisive event for the crystallization of the Sikh Panth" (Singh, 2010: 235). Becoming part of the collective Sikh memory, this event gave rise to the revered institution of martyrdom.

From this point on, involvement with the Mughal state persisted throughout the seventeenth century. At times this involvement was overtly militant, at other times more peaceful and conciliatory. The sixth Guru, Hargobind (r.1606–44) consciously prepared the Sikhs to resist state oppression through military means as and when this became necessary. In contrast to the earlier gurus, Hargobind dressed like a warrior-king girding two swords in place of the woolen rosary. The symbolism of two swords made explicit the principle that had remained implicit in his predecessors, namely, that the Guru commanded both spiritual (*mīrī*) and temporal (*pīrī*) power, as long as the person of the Guru embodied a submission to *hukam*.[25] It was an indication that while power could be harnessed in a different way, ultimately spirituality and politics needed to be unified in the principle of

---

[25] As attested to by Bhaī Gurdās (Vār 1, Paurī 1; Vār 5, Paurī 25; Vār 6, Paurī 1), in addition of course to the compositions of Guru Arjan.

hukam. Over a period of thirty eight years as Guru, Hargobind implemented important defensive measures which laid the basis of the community's militarization. He ordered his Sikhs to train in warfare, built a series of small forts and constructed the Akāl Takht opposite the Harimander for conducting the political and social affairs of the community. The Akāl Takht was more than a physical space, however. It was also an institution which signified the unity of *miri-piri* (spiritual-temporal sovereignty) as embodied by the person of the Guru but even more importantly embodied in the incorporeal principle of *shabad-guru* (Word-as-Guru). In short the Akāl Takht symbolized the sovereignty of Nānak's teaching and the right of the community created by Nānak to determine its own states of affairs.[26]

During the tenure of the seventh Guru, Har Rai (1644–81) and the eighth Guru, Har Krishen (1661–4) overt warfare largely receded, but the ninth Guru, Tegh Bahadur (1664–75) was again forced to confront the increasingly hostile policies of a new emperor Aurangzeb (1658–1707). Aurangzeb rose to power through a similarly brutal war of succession to Jahangir. Once again a Mughal *shahzādha* aligned himself with the powerful Sunni orthodoxy, stoked the fires of Islamic revivalism to ascend to the throne, in the process executing his rivals. During his reign, Aurangzeb enforced strict Islamic laws and taxes, replaced temples with mosques, and implemented an official state policy of nonrecognition of the sovereign existence of non-Muslims, their traditions and way of life. Guru Tegh Bahadur unambiguously (although nonviolently) challenged these policies by openly propagating and proclaiming the sovereignty of Nānak's teaching. The ninth Guru's resistance did not escape state intelligence networks, which conveyed this information to the emperor who duly ordered the Guru's arrest. In circumstances not too dissimilar to those faced by Guru Arjan, charges of sedition were leveled at Tegh Bahadur. Refusing both these charges and the default choice of converting to Islam, he was executed by beheading in Chandni Chowk, Delhi, thereby becoming the second martyr in Sikh history (Grewal, 1996: 46–51).

The preceding Gurus' strategies of resistance culminated in the life and work of the last living Sikh Guru, Gobind Singh (r. 1675–1708). In

---

[26] My narrative broadly follows J. S. Grewal's, *Sikh Ideology, Polity and Social Order*, Delhi: Manohar, p. 26–46.

response to the state's persecution of non-Muslims, the tenth Guru boldly proclaimed a renewal of Guru Nānak's core mission. To put this into effect he undertook a major reorganization of the Sikhs, redefining the core of the community as a religio-military order of spiritual-warriors (or *sant sipāhī*) known as the Khālsā. Personally dedicated to the Guru and outwardly defined by external symbols (the five Ks), the new spiritual-political order was designed to give practical shape to Guru Nānak's principle of sovereign violence ("dying to the Word"). At the same time, it was designed to actively defend the community in the face of increasingly aggressive imperial policies towards those communities the state failed to protect.

Much of Guru Gobind Singh's life was occupied with armed struggle against the emperor's officers and local allies. During the course of these wars all four of his sons were killed and the line of living Gurus came to an end with the tenth Guru's death at the hands of an assassin in 1708. Some months prior to the assassination, Gobind Singh recruited and deputized a militant Vaishnava monk Madho Das (renamed Banda after initiation) to seek justice and retribution on behalf of his two younger sons who were bricked up alive by Wazir Khan, the governor of Sirhind. A few days before his death, Guru Gobind Singh declared the line of living gurus to be at an end and conferred Guruship on the sacred text, renamed Guru Granth Sahib, thereby ensuring that Nānak's teaching and specifically the central organizing concept of *shabad-guru* (the Word as Guru) would remain the sovereign principle (or "eternal" Guru) for the Sikh community.

Line of Flight 1: Martyrdom or Execution?

At first sight, the dominant narrative explaining the Sikh community's evolution from a peaceful path of spiritual endeavor exemplified by the early Sikh Gurus to the path of violence exemplified by the sixth and tenth Gurus, appears to conform to a common sense interpretation of actual events. The facts tell us that the early Sikh Gurus were not involved in physical violence, but several of the later Sikh Gurus definitely were. The most lucid statement of this state of affairs is given by the historian W. H. McLeod in his 1999 book *Sikhism*.

Summarizing a thesis almost three decades in the making, McLeod's explanation stresses that the early Sikh Gurus followed an explicitly "religious path," whose defining characteristic is *nirguṇ bhaktī* – a form of devotion to a transcendent deity resulting in a mystical experience of absolute interiority, which translates on a societal level to a withdrawal from the outside world, a rejection of worldly activity, indifference to politics in favor of peaceful seclusion. McLeod refers to *nirguṇ bhaktī* as the "sant ideal" a term that signifies avoidance of confrontation and involvement in worldly politics. In contrast, according to this line of reasoning, Gurus Hargobind and Gobind Singh involved themselves in worldly politics to such an extent that they essentially deviated from the religious norm (the so-called "sant ideal" or *nirguṇ bhaktī*) established by Guru Nānak. These later Gurus instituted changes, entered worldly politics and resorted to violence as a way of resisting the Mughal state. Consequently, an originally pacifist religion is transformed into a violent religion.

However, as I noted earlier in this Element, this dominant narrative only recognizes violence as external, identifiable either as a visible and recordable event involving battles and bloodshed, or an identifiable agent who causes violence. What remains invisible to this logic of violence is internal or sovereign violence. The invisibility of internal violence is evident in the dominant narrative's treatment of the deaths of Guru Arjan and Tegh Bahadur as nothing more than an execution – the outcome of a state of affairs that was beyond their control, caused by their involvement, however minimal, in affairs of the state. Historians have normally attempted to resolve the issue by digging deeper into source analysis, hoping to prove definitively that it was an execution, or conversely to disprove that it was an act of martyrdom, which tends to become subjective and outside the realm of scientism.

The issue here is not that scholarly reasoning relating to violence is necessarily wrong, or that we must look at it from the perspective of tradition which favors martyrdom. Rather, the point is that the choice we're usually presented (execution versus martyrdom) is both limiting and unproductive because it *not only asks the wrong questions but also keeps in play a dogmatic assumption about the nature of violence*. The logic of violence is beyond the reach of critical reflection because it is already assumed that violence only takes place and is understandable in a *kāl*-centric framework. A more productive approach, argued in the opening section, is to allow normally opposed perspectives (state/community, history/tradition, *kāl/akāl*) to speak to one another, and to assume they are mutually co-implicated. This mutual imbrication brings into view a more holistic, bicameral view of violence presented in Section 1. In other words, it pluralizes the logic of violence, rendering visible internal or sovereign violence that is normally delegitimized by *kāl*-centric/historicist/statist approaches. Of course, this also begs the question: How do we recognize the internal/sovereign violence associated with the killings of the fifth and ninth Gurus?

I would like to answer this question by asking a more productive set of questions in the hope of encouraging readers to think differently about violence. What if we were to avert our gaze from binary oppositions such as execution/martyrdom (with its implication that one is lawful, the other unlawful) and refocus it on the *performative aspect* of the deaths suffered by Arjan and Tegh Bahadur? As noted earlier in this Element, the term "performative" here refers quite simply to movements within the self effected *within* the self (Arjan and Tegh Bahadur) which, in turn, creates change and movement *outside* the subject, but a change that is not necessarily measureable in the timeframe of *kāl*?

But what if the performance itself refers to a mode of "dying to the Word," self-sacrifice or ego-loss, that is to say, a mode of death in which one dies to the self? Such a performance can be described in one sense as a refusal to live and/or a refusal to die in a particular way. Both men were asked to choose a certain kind of life by the state (embrace Islam, or admit to your criminality), which they both refused. In other words, they made a "choice" to not simply die (as we all do!) but to "die to the Word". To recall from Section 1, "Word" is a reference not only to the instruction or teaching of Guru Nānak (*gurbani* or *gurmat*) but for the un-nameable state of consciousness invoked by Nānak, for which he uses the term *nām*. And *nām* is only attainable if one is willing to annihilate one's sense of egotism (*haumai māraṇā*). Accordingly, such a "choice" is not self-willed (*haumai*) but can be made only by killing ego (*haumai marana*). It is therefore an egoless willing, which sounds like an oxymoron, but as we noted earlier, egoless willing is simply *hukam* (cosmic or natural law).[27]

---

[27] For a sustained discussion of these issues, see my *Sikh Philosophy*, Bloomsbury Academic Press, 2022.

The state, of course, will continue to say: "He was guilty, therefore, according to the law, he was executed; he died and this is the end of the matter ... let's move on." From the statist perspective, both Arjan and Tegh Bahadur failed to effect any noticeable change in either the affairs of the state or the general state of affairs of those ruled by the state. This may be why Mughal history does not record any quantitative change as a consequence of their passing. Time simply continues as it was (*kāl*). In contrast, the performativity associated with the deaths of the two Gurus effects a *qualitative* change in the consciousness of those who survive these deaths. By qualitative, I don't necessarily refer to trauma (as an identifiable and therefore external wounding of the ego) although this is certainly part of the broader reception of external violence. Qualitative change refers to self-differentiation, an internal struggle of the self against itself, that registers externally only as the affect of absolute humility. Qualitative change results from the shift in the psychic apparatus when the self refuses attachment to processes of self-preservation in place of "dying to the Word."

Externally, this qualitative movement of affect is registered over a much longer period of time becoming part of the collective memory of a community. And this collective memory in turn becomes a constant repetition/memorialization of the performative "dying to the self." As I will show in the next section of this Element, this repetition-memorialization can also turn into a negative and reactive trauma if the performance is not enacted in accordance to the affect of humility engendered by a "dying to the self/Word." However, when repetition-remembrance occurs positively, for example via *nām simaran*, it effects are registered in a different time-consciousness of *akāl*. In popular Sikh discourse, *akāl* is believed to be a transcendental realm beyond *kāl* (everyday time). If the above argument is correct, however, *akāl* is more usefully envisaged not as beyond time but signaling the limitations of ego. That is to say, as a vastly expanded time-consciousness that subsists in parallel to *kāl*.

From the standpoint of this expanded timeframe (*akāl*) it is possible to glimpse a different logic of violence – a violence that exerts its force primarily through nonviolence. This force is what I have been referring to as sovereign violence – a violence that begins with the struggle of the ego with itself (self-sacrifice) and whose force becomes the ethical touchstone by which any external violence is measured. In short, by, first, "dying to the Word/self" which Nānak also refers to as "playing the game of love," Gurus Arjan and Tegh Bahadur were able to nonviolently resist the state. In other words, in continuity with Nānak's teaching they performed sovereign violence. It is the *nonviolent force* of this sovereign violence that legitimated and empowered the militarization of the Sikhs under Hargobind and Gobind Singh. Consequently, there is no transformation of the Panth from peaceful to violent state – there is only a qualitative movement from one kind of force (internal) to another force (external).

State of Affairs 2: Performing Sovereign Violence 3
Creation of the Khālsā[28]

Alternating strategies of peaceful and militant resistance to the Mughal sultanate fostered by the first nine Gurus culminated in the life and work of

---

[28] The term Khālsā derives from the Arabic *khālis* (lit. pure or unsullied) and the Persian *khālisāh* (a term used during Muslim rule to refer to lands belonging to the crown and administered directly by the king. A variant of the term *Khālsā* appears in a composition of the medieval *bhagat* (Hindi *bhakta*) Kabir, a composition that is included in the Guru Granth Sahib. For Kabir, it would appear that *Khālsā* is coterminous with sant, *bhagat*, i.e., anyone who is able to become self-liberated in contradiction to the Brahmin-mediated path of *karma-kand* specified in the Vedic and Puranic tradition, and also separate from the paths specified by *jogis* and Vaisnhnavism. By the mid- to late seventeenth century, the term "Khālsā" comes to signify *sangats* and individuals directly initiated by one of the Sikh Gurus. For example, Gurus Hargobind and Tegh Bahadur use the term *Khālsā* and its cognate *khalas* to distinguish Sikhs directly initiated by the Gurus themselves from intermediaries such as the *masands*, who by that time had become unreliable. It appears for the first time in one of the *hukamnamas* of Guru Hargobind addressed to an eastern *sangat*, and in a letter by Guru Tegh Bahadur addressing the *sangat* of Patna as his *Khālsā*. Guru Gobind Singh formalized this connection and abolished the order of *masands*, thereby creating a direct link with the Sikh *sangats* and giving the term and gave "Khālsā" a new signification of direct unmediated link with the Guru (see McLeod, 1998; Grewal 2009; Singh, 2005).

the last living Guru, Gobind Singh, who proclaimed a renewal of Guru Nānak's mission by pushing the community towards a full-fledged militarization. He did this by creating the military-religious order of the *Khālsā*. The radicality of this move consisted in externalizing the relationship between violence and spirituality within the body of the community. In this way, the new religio-military order of the *Khālsā* was designed to give practical shape and formal identity to Guru Nānak's central concept of *shabad-guru* and the principle of sovereign violence reflected in the "Word that kills ego."

According to historical Sikh sources,[29] Guru Gobind Singh presents his creation of the *Khālsā* as fulfilling Guru Nānak's mission to uphold the virtue of *dharam* or righteous action.[30] These writings suggest that the Guru reflected deeply on problems besetting the Sikh community, its future and

---

[29] The historical sources pertaining to the *Khālsā*'s creation are relatively light on details and often at variance over exactly what happened. Sainapat's *Sri Guru Sobha*, dated at 1711, remains one of the most important sources. Sainapat was one of the poets in the court of the tenth Guru. But his narrative focuses mainly on the abolition of the *masands* and lacks the descriptive metaphorics of later works in the *Gurbilas* (or heroic) tradition such as Koer Singh's *Gurbilas Patshahi 10*. Koer Singh's version of the creation of the *Khālsā* is part of what might be regarded as traditionalist sources that include Ratan Singh Bhangu's *Prachin Panth Prakash* and Santokh Singh's *Suraj Prakash* and *Gurpratap Suray*, or Giani Gian Singh's *Tawarikh Guru Khālsā*. The version of events presented in this section is based mainly on these last sources, and the traditions of oral exegesis that form part of the contemporary Sikh community's memory. Indeed, this is the way that Sikhs are initiated into the *Khālsā* today and so can be regarded as authoritative. Scholarship that looks at *Khālsā* role in making the Sikh warrior tradition include Purnima Dhavan, *When Sparrows Became Hawks: The Making of the Sikh Warrior Tradition, 1699–1799*, Oxford University Press, 2011; Anne Murphy, *The Materiality of the Past: History & Representation in Sikh Tradition*, New York: Oxford University Press, 2012.

[30] According to J. S. Grewal, "evidence from the Dasam Granth leaves no doubt that Guru Gobind Singh identified himself with his predecessor [Gurus]" and insofar as he often invoked the names of all nine precedinh gurus, was clearly "conscious of his position in the Sikh movement" started by Guru Nānak, as is "reflected in the opening lines of the Sikh Ardas" (Grewal, 2009, p. 22–3).

his own role as Guru. Dissent and disunity were rife, as schismatic sects aided by the Mughal sultanate continued to challenge his authority as Guru. But the central problem as he saw it, consisted ironically, in the *personal* nature of guruship. If, as Nānak had taught, the source of sovereign authority was the impersonal principle of *satguru* = word = *shabad-guru*, then perhaps the time had arrived to abolish the line of personal succession altogether? But to replace it with what? And how would the unified concept of *mīrī-pīrī* – the sovereign as temporal-spiritual – be embodied in the absence of a living guru?

The solution as Guru Gobind Singh saw it was to actualize Guru Nānak's sovereign violence by incarnating the concept of *shabad-guru* ("dying to the Word") in the body of the community. To put these nascent ideas into effect he requested his followers to congregate at Anandpur for the Baisaikhi festival of 1699. On the evening of March 30, 1699, in front of a large crowd, he *performatively enacted* Guru Nānak's central teaching about the relationship between sovereignty and violence. Sikh writers have retold the spectacle as the performance of a three-part drama heavily layered with mystical and political resonances and divided into three separate acts (see Figures 1, 2, and 3), just as if it were a theatre performance. The three scenes of the drama are as follows: *Scene 1:* The Willing Sacrifice; *Scene 2:* Initiation of the Double Edged Sword; *Scene 3:* Immolation of the god-king:[31]

Scene 1: The Willing Sacrifice

Brandishing a sword, the Guru came of a tent and asked the crowd if there was one among them willing to sacrifice his or her head for the Guru (see Figure 2). The call was repeated several times until one Sikh eventually stepped forward and offered his head. The Guru took the hapless victim into the tent, from where a loud thud was heard, suggesting the victim's decapitation. This process was then repeated until five Sikhs had offered their heads. After a short time, the guru came out of the tent with the five

---

[31] A beautiful rendering of this three-stage drama can be found in Nikky Singh's *The Birth of the Khālsā*, New York: SUNY, 2005.

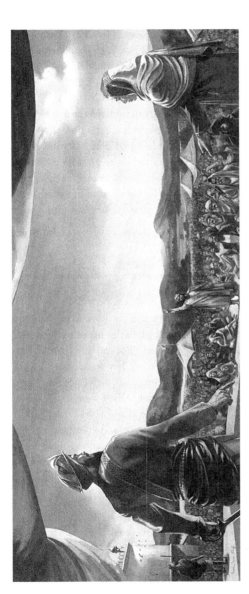

Figure 2 *Vaisakhi: Birth of the Khalsa* (Artist: Kanwar Singh Dhillon)

willing victims all dressed in blue and saffron robes. They were introduced to the *sangat* as the Guru's five beloved ones (or *panj piare*) and the nucleus of a new sovereign order called *Khālsā* (Singh, 2005; Mandair, 2013).

Scene 2: Initiation of the Double-Edged Sword

In the second part of this strange drama, the Guru initiated the five beloved ones into the new order of the *Khālsā* by implementing a new rite called *khande-ka-pahul* (nectar of the double-edged sword). Placing water sweetened with sugar crystals into an iron vessel and stirred it with a double-edged sword while reciting the hymns *Japjī*, *Jaap*, *Anand*, *Swayai*, and *Chaupai*. The resulting nectar, called *amrit* (lit. the elixir of life-death) was then administered to the five neophytes (see Figure 3). As it was sprinkled in their eyes and hair each was asked to repeat:

waheguru ji ka Khālsā, waheguru ji ki fateh

> The *Khālsā* belongs to the true Guru (*waheguru*), to the Guru belongs the victory.

The Guru then asked each of the initiates in turn to drink from the same vessel, signifying a dissolution of all social boundaries between them, and their rebirth into a new form of association. To seal this part of the ceremony, the Guru told them that from then on they were to break with their family names and adopt a new name: Singh for men (meaning lion), and Kaur for women (meaning princess). Finally, they were given a new code of conduct. They were to carry on their body five *kakār* or five Ks:[32] (i) *kēsh* or long uncut hair signifying one's connection and affirmation of the law of nature; (ii) *kangā* a comb to keep the hair clean and intact, also signifying an affirmation of the householder's life, and a rejection of asceticism; (iii) *kirpān* a dagger or short sword signifying the right to bear

---

[32] The earliest *Rahitnamas* do not prescribe the five Ks, and mention no more than two or three of the Ks. For example Sainapati's *GurSobha* mentions the need for *Khālsā* initiates to wear long uncut hair (*kesh*) and to bear arms (*kirpān*). Some historians have argued that the full five Ks, as well as the issue of naming (Singh/Kaur) may be a later development, probably in the early to mid- eighteenth century.

Figure 3 *Khande-ka-pahul* Initiation. Artist unknown.

arms as well as a strict moral duty to protect all life; (iv) *kaṛā*: an iron bracelet signifying one's being bound within *hukam*; (v) *kacch* or short breeches signifying the need for restraint. These five Ks were to be worn as bodily signifiers marking a *Khālsā* as different from others, one who could not hide in difficult circumstances, and as a householder who lived by a certain discipline. In addition to the five Ks they were given a set of moral injunctions to adhere to (Singh, 2014: 105–72).

To all intents and purposes, the initiation ceremony seemed to be complete. For through this new ceremony, the neophytes had severed all allegiance to previous caste occupations (*krit nās*), to family ties (*kul nās*), and to previous creeds (*dharam nās*), in addition to rituals not sanctioned by the Sikh way of life. But the drama was by no means over!

Scene 3: The Guru's Self-Immolation

Immediately after initiating the *panj piare* or five beloved ones, Guru Gobind Rai again surprised the congregation. He dropped to his knees in front of the *panj piare* and begged them to initiate him into the *Khālsā*. At first, the *panj piare* were taken aback and refused, saying that he was the Guru and they were his Sikhs. How could a disciple initiate the master? But when the Guru pleaded for initiation, they relented and administered the *amrit* to Gobind Rai in exactly the same way. By receiving *amrit*, the Guru also became a *Khālsā* and relinquished his caste and kinship name (Rai/Sodhi) and became Guru Gobind Singh (see Figure 4).

Although this seemed like a radical gesture, the congregation quickly realized that the Guru had not really done anything new in this final act. The Sikh community had witnessed this performance before – nine times as a matter of fact! Guru Nānak himself had performed the same act, performing a self-immolation in order to become the disciple of Guru Angad, who in turn went from being Nānak's disciple to Nānak's Guru. And so on with the other Gurus until this moment.

In the same way that the first Nānak had performatively harnessed the concept of sovereign violence to transmit the authority of guruship, so the tenth Nānak (Gobind Singh) was dramatizing the same concept by transmitting sovereign authority to the *Khālsā*. From this moment on the principle was established that the five *Khālsā* Sikhs could represent the entire community and initiate other Sikhs into the order of the *Khālsā*.

Line of Flight-2: Economies of Violence in the Khālsā *Myth*[33]

What is the *Khālsā* narrative all about? From the standpoint of historicism, the *Khālsā* simply fulfilled the need for a more concrete identity that remained implicit in early Sikh tradition. Historicism can only see

---

[33] The discussion below is a revised version of "Excursus 2" in *Sikhism: A Guide For the Perplexed*, 2013, pp. 63–6.

Figure 4 Self-Immolation: The Guru receives initiation as Khalsa [Artist: Kirpal Singh]

the *Khālsā*'s bearing of arms as a violation of the sacred, by deviating from the seemingly peaceful path of the earlier Gurus, thus interfering in questions of sovereignty that are matters for the state, Mughal or otherwise.

A more productive approach is to see the *Khālsā* narrative as a radical reconceptualization of the relationship between violence and sovereignty, where the three scenes teach us how Guru Nānak's sovereign violence repeats itself in a different context. To take this seriously, however, we need to think about the relationship between violence and the sacred in terms of the central theme in the three scenes, namely, *self*-sacrifice or ego-loss. Thus in scenes 1 and 2, the Guru demanded a victim willing to sacrifice herself: "I want a head." In this demand-imperative-command, there is an implicit violence (Violence 1). The demand for sacrifice is followed by a decision by the neophyte to risk what is most precious to him or her, namely, one's life. This decision is the source of ethical responsibility, where responsibility means to respond to the call of death willingly, to give up what is seemingly one's ownmost. But the sacrificial demand also happens at another level, namely, where the neophyte is asked to sacrifice his/her social identity (ego) by breaking with social frameworks. We can designate this violence towards the symbolic framework (and therefore the self) as Violence 2. Here, the Guru also returns their lives by: (i) presenting their bodies to the *sangat* and (ii) giving them a new, unfettered identity, a new community.

Yet Violence 1 and Violence 2 are not necessarily unique. We can see them at play in other forms of initiation, religious or otherwise. The real difference of the *Khālsā* narrative resides in scene 3, where the tenth Guru dramatizes Nānak's concept of sovereign violence by reversing the initiation ceremony. That the Guru begged to be initiated as a disciple (*chela*) of the five beloved ones (*panj piare*), and merged into the ranks of the commons is an exercise not simply in humility, but a *performative deconstruction of ego-based sovereignty*, the enactment of a certain kind of democracy in which the Guru donates power (*jōr/kratos*) to the common people (*lōk/demos*) by emptying his divinity/kingship, by negating his transcendental status. This donation of power to the undercommons through willing sacrifice of the divine (a variation on the "death of God") can be seen as a violence committed by the divine to its own divinity, such that it actively wills to relinquish its divinity. This would be a third violence, Violence 3, where the sacred manifests sovereignty by relinquishing self-attachment.

In other words, the *Khālsā* is a sovereign entity but *its sovereignty depends not on the accumulation of ego but on interior excessive violence associated with ego-loss*. While the first two forms of violence balance themselves out and maintain an economy of violence, the third form, however, constitutes an excessive violence where the Guru sacrifices his transcendence/authority and therefore does violence to the very order of sacredness, and empowers the *Khālsā*. Thus, Violence 3 (the violence of sacred death = renunciation or ego-loss) exceeds the first two forms of violence and shatters any possible economy, making the *Khālsā* an embodiment of sovereign violence. It is this excessiveness of ego-loss that authorizes the *Khālsā* to deploy violence and therefore to govern itself. Guru Gobind Singh's creation of *Khālsā* is grounded in the giving of a gift without return, which is the only economy of sacrifice (or self-loss).

This traditionalist understanding of the *Khālsā* myth presents a startling conclusion about the meaning of (non)violence and therefore the much misunderstood relationship between Guru Nānak and Guru Gobind Singh. Was the formalization of violence as a religio-political order really a transformation of the earlier Panth of Guru Nānak? The answer is both yes and no! While the actors and the circumstances are different from the time of Guru Nānak, and the Panth is given a form it did not possess at the time of the early Sikh Gurus, the *intensity of the concept of violence* – and therefore its underpinning philosophy – remains practically the same. In other words, the sacrificial economy that gives rise to the *Khālsā* is qualitatively the same sacrificial economy that Guru Nānak enacted, on the one hand, through his sovereign experience of absolute self-surrender or ego-loss while remaining in the world, and, on the other hand, in transferring Guruship to Angad. That is, in order to transfer guruship to Angad, Nānak had to become Angad's disciple, and in order to become his disciple he had to become a Sikh and absolutely surrender his "divinity" to the *satguru*. This involved qualitatively the same economy of violence to the self (ego-loss) that created the *Khālsā*.

The clear implication is that Guru Nānak was not in any way less "violent" than Guru Gobind Singh? If the true meaning of violence is first and foremost a struggle with oneself, a struggle with one's ego, then violence is inseparable from spirituality. The caveat, however, is that the Khālsā's access to power remains legitimate only if it remains true to Guru Nānak's and Guru Gobind Singh's sovereign principle: the constant need to live in accordance with *hukam* – the constant remembrance of absolute self-surrender. Once the Panth forgets this paradoxical principle or allows this particular capacity to be captured or compromised, it self-destructs. As we see in the remaining sections, this happened time and again as the community evolved after the death of Guru Gobind Singh.

States of Affairs 3: Warfare and Violence in the Colonial Period

From Guerilla Operations to a Standing *Khālsā* Army

In the years immediately after Guru Gobind Singh's death (1708), one of his handpicked deputies, a former Vaishnava ascetic named Banda Bahadur, led a number of uprisings against the Mughal state sacking cities such as Sirhind. In spite of some successes, he was eventually captured and publically executed in Delhi. For the next two decades, the remaining *Khālsā* forces were hunted almost to extinction.

But the balance of power was shifting against the Mughal empire, which had been weakened by fighting on too many fronts and repeated incursions by Afghan invaders. Emboldened by this, the *Khālsā* forces continued to operate a form of guerilla warfare, roving the countryside in small bands, plundering and harassing the authorities and their supporters whenever opportunities arose. By the 1740s, the small bands had developed into independent militia-based confederacies called *misls*, with each *misl* led by a chieftain and held together by kinship ties. Combinations of larger *misls* were called *dal Khālsā* and unified under the command of a chosen leader for strategic engagements (Grewal, 1990: 92–3).

The success of the *misl* system enabled *Khālsā* membership to grow considerably by the closing decades of the eighteenth century. Part of this success owed to the *misls* being able to retain occupied territories and establish a firmer footing in the Punjab heartlands. However, the loose political unity of the *misls* lasted only as long as they were confronted by a tangible enemy. With the Afghan invaders gone and Mughal power in terminal decline, the *misls* began to fight one another for control of territory. The eventual winner of this internecine conflict was the Sukerchakia *misl* led by its ambitious leader Ranjit Singh. Within a decade, Ranjit Singh had absorbed the main *misls* under his control, established Lahore as his capital and later added the territories of Multan, Kashmir, and Peshawar, effectively creating a sovereign Sikh kingdom, and giving himself the title of supreme ruler or maharajah of Punjab.

From the 1790s until his death in 1839, Ranjit Singh spent a great deal of effort building up a technically advanced, disciplined army modelled on European techniques of drill and warfare. During Ranjit Singh's four decades of rule, Punjab entered a period of stability and prosperity where *Khālsā* forces became a dominant military and political power. Soon after his death, however, Ranjit Singh's court descended into chaos and confusion sparked by struggles for succession among his heirs, and partly by the steady encroachment of the British imperial machine into Punjab. Within a decade of Ranjit Singh's death, the Sikh kingdom was drawn into full-scale military conflict with the British, known as the Anglo-Sikh wars (1845–9). By 1849, the Sikh kingdom was annexed into the British empire and the Sikhs had entered into the harsh realities of European colonial rule.

Constructing the Sikhs as a "Martial Race"

Immediately after the Anglo-Sikh wars, the *Khālsā* army was disbanded and Punjab demilitarized as Sikhs who had served with Ranjit Singh were required to publicly surrender their weapons and return to civilian life. However, this policy was quickly reversed for two reasons. First, there was a significant body of research writings by Indologists and military officers that regarded the Sikhs as a "new and peculiar nation" politically distinct from Hindus and Muslims (Malcolm, 1812: 144; Cunningham, 1849: 79). Second, prominent British officers such as Colin Campbell, Henry Havelock, and John Lawrence extolled the prowess of the Sikhs during the Anglo-Sikh wars. As the first Governor General of Punjab, Lawrence saw "immense value in harnessing Sikh martiality" given the strategic position of Punjab in view of threats from Russia, the Afghans, and other tribes hostile to British rule (Ballantyne, 2006: 44–9). A regular flow of articles in influential newspapers began to paint a picture of Punjabi Sikhs as possessing sturdy physique and masculine values in comparison with the more "effeminate" Hindustanis. Such attributions tended to fit well into an influential racial discourse centered on the superiority of Northern (Aryan-Caucasian) races and their suitability for the military (Fox, 1990; Streets, 2011).

By the mid-1850s and certainly by the time of the "Indian Mutiny" (1857–8) large numbers of Sikhs were recruited into the British imperial army. Regiments led by Havelock, Campbell, and Lawrence contained large numbers of Sikhs whose loyalty and military skills were noted with aplomb (Streets, 2011: 69–72). As Lawrence reflected: "But for the fidelity of the Sikhs every vestige of European civilization, would in all probability, have been eradicated" (Ballantyne, 2006: 64). After 1858, British recruitment policy shifted towards Punjab as the "home of the most martial races of India and [is] the nursery of our best soldiers" (Ballantyne, 2006: 46–64). For the next three decades, British media correspondences from army officers highlighted the exploits of military men who had saved the empire from untimely demise.

As Heather Streets has argued, stories crafted by media focused on three groups of soldiers who were linked together as "representatives of collective military heroism: Highland Scots, Punjabi Sikhs and Nepalese Gurkhas. Stories that celebrated their valor and ferocity and gallantry articulated new connections between British soldiers and the most loyal Indian soldiers, and between military service in the empire, ideal masculinity and racial superiority" (Streets, 2011: 52). By the 1870s, Sikhs and Highlanders were routinely linked in some of the most compelling tales about the "Indian Mutiny." A kind of mythic connection was forged between these two groups representing two sides of a hypermasculine militarism. As these tropes of race, religion, and masculinity were repeated over and again, the connection between images of these two exemplary martial races – kilted Highlanders and turbaned Sikhs – came to be seen as natural (Streets, 2011: 50–1).

Anti-Colonial Violence and Nonviolence

By the opening decade of the twentieth century, rapport between Sikhs and the British turned to outright hostility as the colonizers turned a blind eye towards famines, plagues, and rampant farmer indebtedness and suicide. Widespread disaffection led to the formation of two different anticolonial Sikh nationalist movements: the Gadhr *lehar* (primarily a diasporic movement led by Sikh emigres on the Canadian West coast) and the Akāli Dal, which defined itself in explicitly "religious" terms (Singh, 1966: 151–216).

The Gadhr movement channeled its anticolonialism into a transnational movement advocating violent resistance to British rule. Its workers were sent back to Punjab to incite anarchic revolution (*gadhr*) against British rule. Although it managed to incite a few uprisings, the movement was thwarted by a well-informed British and Canadian intelligence network and was widely seen as a failure. Its historical importance lies in the fact that it spawned a variety of related movements including the Babbar Akālis, an armed faction of the Punjab Communist Party known as the Naxalites, as well as a transnational Sikh diasporic network actively used in the late twentieth century by Sikh militant movements demanding an independent Sikh state called Khalistan (see next section).

In April 1919, over 400 mainly Sikh civilians were massacred by British troops after they had gathered at Jalianwala Bagh (Amritsar) to listen to speeches. The massacre prompted the creation of a new and more radical party to represent interests of the Sikh peasant classes who had grown impatient with Sikh elites who in turn had gained a reputation as 'toadies' of the British colonial administration. Although no less radical than the Gadhr movement, the Akāli party drew from the tradition of nonviolent resistance associated with Sikh martyrdom and self-sacrifice. In doing so, it opened an era of nonviolent political agitation, initially against British rule, but also against the postcolonial Indian state in the 1970s and 1980s (Uberoi, 1996: 114).

The Akālis' basic mandate was to free Sikh shrines from the inherited custodianship of *mahants*, many of whom were backed by the British. The mandate was put into effect by coordinating groups of volunteers known as *shahīdī jathās* (sacrificial units) to take control of the shrines (p. 98). Between 1921 and 1925, the Akālis successfully liberated a number of historic shrines in a campaign closely monitored by Mohandas Gandhi – the icon of antiviolent resistance in the twentieth century. By the end of the five year struggle to liberate Sikh gurdwaras, over 4,000 Akālis had died, over 2,000 were wounded, and 30,000 men and women were jailed. However, the prolonged nonviolent struggle ultimately forced the British to sign a bill, the Sikh Gurdwaras Act (1925), formally recognizing the SGPC as legally authorized to control and manage Sikh Gurdwaras (Singh, 2009: 193–214).

Lines of Flight 2: Capturing and Performing Sovereign Violence 4

In this section, we have surveyed four different formations: the *misls*, Ranjit Singh's standing army, the *Khālsā* soldiers of the British Imperial Army, and the Akālis. All four were involved in violence in one way or another and are regarded by most Sikhs as ways in which the *Khālsā* core principle of sovereign violence was actualized. The question, however, is whether and to what extent these four different formations truly performed sovereign violence or were doing something altogether different?

A detailed answer to this question is outside the scope of the Element. Nevertheless, I'd like to complete this line of flight with a series of questions and conjectures rather than any conclusive answers. Is it possible, for example, to discern broadly distinct *orientations* of violence at work in these *Khālsā* formations – orientations attributable in turn to an ethical disjuncture between the *Khālsā* ideal and its actualization on the ground?

In this vein, it might be suggested, for example, that both Ranjit Singh's standing army and the *Khālsā* formation constructed by the British as a "martial race," far from performing sovereign violence, were, in fact, formations engineered to *capture* sovereign violence. By "capture," I refer to ways in which the *Khālsā*'s *akāl*-centrism is replaced by a *kāl*-centric ethos. Loyalty (in the sense of one's understanding of sovereignty) is transferred from an ego-annihilating internal practice to an ego-centric external identity geared to the service of a new state – the territorial Sikh kingdom in the case of Ranjit Singh, or the units of *Khālsā* soldiery now loyal to the British imperial state.

In recent years, certain Sikh advocacy groups have generated much information and discussion by resurrecting the martial aspect of Sikhism and its potential to be of service to the British state or the American state in the twenty-first century. The information generated by these groups have idealized both Ranjit Singh and the British army as a doyens of the *Khālsā* principle. Closer examination, however, suggests that Ranjit Singh undermined the democratic principle of the *Khālsā* by abolishing the *gurumatta* institution (where different *Khālsā* factions and individuals used to meet to make collective decisions) in order to secure his own autocratic rule. *Khālsā* rule under Ranjit Singh is therefore something of a myth. In the case of the British, the Sikhs could only be incorporated into the imperial army by subverting their *akāl*-centrism.

From this perspective, the Akāli agitation against the British is doubly interesting. On the one hand, by resorting to a nonviolent agitation the Akālis appear to have rediscovered and put into play the sovereign violence of the *Khālsā* ideal. Their practice of sending *shahīdī jathās* to court arrest and elicit a violent response by the British was done in the spirit both of Guru Arjan and Tegh Bahadur's martyrdoms and *Khālsā* militancy, by offering no physical violence against the British, even though all their *jathas* marched fully armed with *kirpān*s or similar weapons. The icon of non-violent anticolonial resistance, Mohandas Gandhi, found it rather difficult to comprehend. His speeches about the Akāli campaigns between 1921 and 1925 reveal a clear and unambiguous distinction between his own notion of nonviolence and the Akāli practice derived from their Sikh heritage. Gandhi was nervous that, being fully armed, the Akālis would not be able to resist the temptation to retaliate with violence if they were attacked (as they often were) thereby jeopardizing the broader anticolonial struggle. In contra-distinction from Gandhi's legalistic definition of nonviolence, the Akālis derived their practice from Guru Nānak's sovereign violence incarnate in the *Khālsā* body, according to which violence is not opposed to nonviolence but intrinsically connected to it. Gandhi felt compelled to keep reminding the Akālis to stay on the non-violent track despite the differences between their respective attitudes:

> One of the telegrams received by me tells me that the *jatha* was and remained throughout strictly non-violent. You have, from the very commencement, claimed that your movement is perfectly non-violent and religious. I would like every one of us to understand all the implications of non-violence . . . *I am not unaware of the fact that non-violence is not your creed. It is therefore doubly incumbent on you to guard against any violence in thought or word creeping in the movement.* (Gandhi, 1958: 211, emphasis added).

4 "1984": Clash of Sovereignties?

States of Affairs 4 (kāl)

Nonviolent Resistance Confronts Indian State Violence

After the partition of India in 1947, Sikhs found themselves in a precarious political position. Demographically, they constituted a significant minority but could not exercise any degree of self-determination as the 1925 Sikh Gurdwaras Act designated Sikhs a "religious" minority. This had the effect of politically marginalizing them, allowing the Indian National Congress (INC) to exploit this weakness. Unlike the Akālis, the INC had reconstructed itself as an overtly secular party in the 1930s. The INC did this by ideologically transitioning from the Gandhian position of communitarian nationalism to a European-style secular nationalism, thereby giving itself a legal monopoly for separating religion from state. From that point onwards, the Akāli position would be limited to the politics of religious identity even though the Akālis tried to project an ostensibly secular stance based on cross-community cultural factors such as linguistic identity.

Once the boundaries of Punjab were redrawn along linguistic lines in 1966, the Akālis were able to form a government but unable to exercise power without interference from the Congress Party, now led by Indira Gandhi, whose main priority was to centralize power and keep the Hindu vote bank appeased. The government's seeming indifference towards provincial issues led to wide-ranging civil disobedience campaigns throughout the country, in response to which Indira Gandhi declared an Emergency in 1975, thus effectively stalling the democratic process. In alliance with other political groups, the Akālis spearheaded a series of *morchas* (nonviolent protests) in which over 40,000 Akālis courted arrest, including many of its leadership. After the Emergency was withdrawn in 1977, the Congress was routed at the polls and the Akālis were able to form a coalition government. But any gains made by the Akālis during these years were quickly reversed when Indira Gandhi returned to power in 1980.

Between 1980 and 1983, a familiar struggle ensued between the Akālis and the Congress, but by this time the political stakes had risen sharply as many Sikhs began to revive ideas about autonomy. In July 1981, the Akālis launched yet another major nonviolent agitation for Sikh rights, interestingly termed *dharam yudh morcha* or "war/agitation for justice." In response, Indira Gandhi adopted different tactics partly because Congress now faced a more potent threat to its electoral base at the national and provincial levels. This threat came from the return of Hindu nationalist movements into the political arena in the late 1970s, which had successfully reorganized the Hindu networks along religious lines and unified the vast Hindu vote bank against the secular Congress through stigmatization of non-Hindu minorities. Confronted by minorities such as the Sikhs, Muslims, and Communists at the provincial level, and by the rise of Hindu fundamentalism at the national level, Indira Gandhi was caught in a serious dilemma. While Muslims and Dalits were part of an important vote bank for Congress, they could not afford to alienate mainstream Hindus who comprised the vast majority of Indian voters and were increasingly being affected by a stridently anti-Muslim rhetoric of Hindu religious nationalism (Mandair, 2009: 301–4).

"Systemic Violence": Recasting of Sikhs as the "Internal Enemy"

Indira Gandhi and her Congress policymakers' solution to this dilemma was to divert the attention of the Hindu voting bloc through a threefold strategy of: (i) derailing the Akāli Dal's ostensibly secular and nonviolent stance; (ii) promoting fringe elements within the Sikh community; (iii) deploying state-owned media to refashion the image of Sikhs as the internal enemy of the Indian nation (Grewal, 2009). The overall effect of this three-pronged approach was that it enabled Congress to recast the Sikhs as an internal threat to Indian national unity by generating an image of "subjective violence" about Sikhs and Sikhism (Žižek, 2007: chapter 1).

As noted in Section 1, subjective violence is the visible form of violence designed to create a spectacle. The term *subjective* suggests several markers that tell us something about the nature of the violence in question: that it is performed by a clearly identifiable agent: the "fundamentalist," the "terrorist," the religious nationalist, and so on; that it has clearly identifiable consequences: ethno-religious cleansing, civil unrest, sectarian or communal rioting, international conflict, violent insurgency, and so on; and that the violent actions of the agent conform to a certain logic that is intrinsic to the formation and maintenance of identity (Žižek, 2007: 1–3).

The conflict between the Sikhs and the secular Indian state from the late 1970s to the 1990s exemplifies all of these markers. A legacy of this conflict was the branding of Sikhism as a "violent religion" by mainstream media in India and the West. The image of Sikh militants as turbaned fundamentalists carrying AK-47s and its comparison to the rising phenomenon of "Islamic violence" (in the style of the Iranian revolution and the Afghan Mujahadeen) made life rather uncomfortable for minority Sikh communities in the West and outside Punjab in India. Several high-profile actions by Sikh militant groups or those claiming to act in the name of Sikh militancy – including the hijacking and bombing of civilians buses in North India, the hijacking of an Indian Airlines plane in 1983, the annual spectacle of Sikhs burning the Indian flag outside Indian embassies, the assassinations of Indian politicians including an Indian prime minister, and, perhaps most notoriously, the 1986 mid-air explosion of an Air India plane carrying over 300 passengers just off the coast of Ireland – all helped to manufacture subjective violence embodied by the "Sikh terrorist."

As Richard Mann observes the Indian media at the time were instrumental in creating "a recurring stereotype of a fanatical religious figure who is a threat to the integrity of the Indian state" and became a means to "justify the horrific violence of the state against Sikhs" (Mann, 2016: 116). Indeed, the "danger of such stereotypes and the media framing of events," according to Mann, "prevents the dissemination of accurate accounts of events, issues and individuals and instead become tools of the state to mask their own violence against minority groups" (Mann, 2016: 117). Since this conflict is reasonably well documented elsewhere,[34] I briefly highlight

---

[34] See, for example Gurharpal Singh, *Ethnic Conflict in India: A Case-Study of Punjab* (New York: Macmillan Publishers, 2000); Sanjib Baruah, ed., *Ethno-nationalist Movements in India* (New Delhi: Oxford University Press, 2009); Rajiv Kapur, *Sikh Separatism: The Politics of Faith* (London: Allen and Unwin, 1986); Ghani Jaffar, *The Sikh Volcano* (Lahore: Vikas Publishing House, 1982).

subjective violence in terms of key events, agents, and agencies associated with it.[35]

Rise of Bhindranwale

The promotion of fringe groups by the center government undermined the Akāli Dal's putatively secular stance and engineered sectarian violence as well as attacks on the Punjab police and right-wing Hindu organizations.

Arguably the single most important fringe figure was Sant Jarnail Singh Bhindranwale, the charismatic head cleric of Damdami Taksaal, known for his fiery rhetoric and uncompromising stance towards the excesses of the Punjab police and Hindu nationalists. Within a short time, Bhindranwale became the most identifiable figure in the rise of Sikh militancy. But by early 1982, Bhindranwale had joined forces with the Akālis and turned his energy towards a full scale confrontation with the ruling Congress Party who had cynically allowed the law and order situation in Punjab to deteriorate to dangerous levels, allowing robberies, hijackings, and murders to take place (often pinning these on Sikhs to discredit the Akāli image). At the same time, the police were given sweeping powers of arrest and harassment. Working seemingly in tandem with Congress policy, Indian media, and some Indian academics, exacerbated tensions between Hindus and Sikhs, routinely portraying the situation as a "Hindu–Sikh conflict."[36]

To make matters worse, Indira Gandhi imposed Presidential rule on Punjab in October 1983 bringing into force an ordinance known as the Punjab Disturbed Areas Act. This act, which remained in place until 1994, empowered police and paramilitary officials to "fire upon or otherwise use force, even to the causing of death, against any person acting in contravention of any law" (Axel, 2001: 131). Acting with legal impunity, the police and armed forces institutionalized a kind of identification system in which the *amritdhari* body (the body of Khālsā-initiated Sikhs) was marked

---

[35] For a useful overview of these issues, see Grewal, 2009: 287–314.

[36] A good example of such bias is Rajiv A. Kapoor's 1986 *Sikh Separatism: The Politics of Faith*. This book, like most others of that period, present the conflict as entirely "communal," sparked and driven by religious fundamentalism, rather than taking a critical approach to the Indian state's central role in the entire affair.

out both as the terrorist subject and as the object of systemic police brutality. As outlined in a training manual that kept police and soldiers informed about terrorist operations: "Any knowledge of the Amritdharis who are dangerous people and pledged to commit murder, arson and acts of terrorism should immediately be brought to the notice of authorities. These people may appear harmless from the outside but they are basically committed to terrorism ... Their identity and whereabouts must be disclosed" (Axel, 2001: 132). As Brian Axel notes: "[B]y the 1990's, it seems, the identification of *amritdharis* as terrorists had become well established in police discourse. As one officer stated: 'A profile was developed of who was considered to be anti-government and pro-Khalistan. Based on that profile, young Sikh men between the ages of eighteen and forty, who have long beards and wear turbans, are considered to be pro-Khalistan'" (Axel, 2001: 131–2).

In response to this increasingly dangerous situation, Bhindranwale campaigned in the villages of Punjab, addressing audiences and combining the roles of religious cleric and political critic. In addition to addressing rampant problems of drug and alcohol addiction (to which the state turned a blind eye), he urged Sikhs not only to become *amritdhari* (those initiated into *Khālsā*) but insisted that each *amritdhari* should be *shastardhari* (a weapon bearer) to protect themselves from the state's excesses. For Bhindranwale, the choice of weapons was not confined to the obligatory *kirpān* (short sword) worn as part of the five Ks. He extended the bearing of arms to modern weaponry and machinery:

> For every village you should keep one motorcycle, three *amritdharis* and three guns. These are not meant for killing innocent people. For a Sikh to have arms and kill an innocent person is a serious sin. But, Khālsā ji, to have arms and not to procure your legitimate rights is an even bigger sin. It is for you to decide how to use these arms.
>
> (*Bhindranwale, Speeches*, Sandhu, 1999)

Bhindranwale was given excessive coverage by the state-run Indian media to the extent that his presence soon overshadowed that of the Akālis. When quizzed by journalists about his stance on a separate Sikh state (Khalistan), he replied "I am neither in favor of it nor against. If they give it to us, we won't say no," which was, in effect, a warning to the Akāli leaders not to betray Sikh demands for greater autonomy (Grewal, 2009: 287–314).

As Punjab politics became more polarized, Bhindranwale joined forces with the Akālis creating a common front to oppose Congress. But early in 1984 Bhindranwale broke with the Akālis and took up residence with his followers at the Akāl Takht, Sikhism's seat of political sovereignty, a move that was calculated, on the one hand, to undermine the Akāli Dal's monopoly on political and religious authority within Sikhism and, on the other hand, to invite a violent attack on the Akāl Takht by the state. Part of Bhindranwale's calculation was that any attack on the Akāl Takht would constitute an attack on Sikh political sovereignty and would thus engineer a clash of sovereignties, thereby exposing a fundamental flaw within the institution of Indian secular democracy. Using the Akāl Takht as a base, Bhindranwale spearheaded a more extreme phase of resistance to the state including acts of retributive violence, assassinations of police officers and others deemed to be "enemies of Sikhism." Between March and June 1984, there was a tense standoff between Bhindranwale in the Akāl Takht and state paramilitary forces who had surrounded the Golden Temple complex with a view to curtail Bhindranwale's activities (Mandair, 2013: 98–104).

This prompted Indira Gandhi to remove Bhindranwale from the Golden Temple complex through a massive army operation codenamed Blue Star and fronted by Sikh battalions. In June 1984, the Indian Prime Minister ordered the army to take positions within the Golden Temple complex, with all transportation and phone communication links cut on June 3 thereby isolating Punjab from and preventing all journalistic reporting. Thirty-seven other gurdwaras in Punjab were also surrounded by army forces. A full-scale military attack on the Akāl Takht commenced on June 5. Tragically, the military assault, codenamed Operation Blue Star, took place on the martyrdom anniversary of Guru Arjan, a day when the Golden Temple complex was filled with pilgrims visiting from around the world. During three days of intense fighting, the government forces encountered fierce resistance from Bhindranwale's followers. The army incurred heavy losses and in the thick of the fighting destroyed historical buildings including the Sikh reference library, which housed relics of Sikh history and important manuscripts. More than 4,000 people were killed as a result of the attack.

In October 1984, Indira Gandhi was assassinated by her Sikh body-guards, which, in turn, was followed by anti-Sikh pogroms in New Delhi. The period from 1984 to 1992 saw (a) the emergence and pro-liferation of a militant Sikh insurgency within and outside India for a separate Sikh state (Khalistan) and (b) a series of massive counter-insurgency operations by Indian paramilitary forces that systematically eliminated the "terrorist" threat and returned Punjab to a state of normalcy in the early 1990s.

Lines of Flight 3 (akāl)

The *Un*timely in "1984": Performing Sovereign Violence 5

Although the "1984" episode has been relatively well documented by journalists, scholars, and activists, and in spite of a sitting Indian prime minister's "Gandhian moment of clarity" for finding the courage to apol-ogize for the Congress Party's role,[37] many remain perplexed by the fact that the intensity of emotions associated with "1984" appear not to have abated with the passage of time. Some scholars have pointed to the styles and politics of memorialization, particularly on the part of Sikh nationalists, in keeping this intensity alive by locating the event in a long tradition of martyrdoms and martyrologies.[38] Others point out that the political issues that caused "1984" have not been addressed.[39]

While this is all true, there is something else, something that exceeds factual, data-oriented analyses of 1984. This elusive aspect, I would argue, has something to do with the paradoxical nature of sovereign violence that we have been exploring throughout this Element, something that remains irreducible to being empirically analyzed. In the 1984 episode, there lies an

---

[37] www.thehindu.com/news/the-india-cables/Manmohan-Singhs-apology-for-anti-Sikh-riots-a-lsquoGandhian-moment-of-moral-clarity-says-2005-cable/article14692805.ece

[38] See Radhika Chopra, *Sikh Formations*, Vol. 9, No. 2 and Vol. 11, No.3.

[39] Jasdev S. Rai, *Sikh Formations*, Vol. 7, No.1, pp. 1–41.

unquantifiable aspect corresponding to sovereign violence as I have described it in earlier sections. As a way of concluding this Element, and in a sense that may surprise some readers, I argue that the importance of the 1984 episode may lie not in the fine details of what *actually* happened (for example, the Indian state's defeat of "Sikh terrorism"), but in something that remains inexpressible, namely, the expression of a mode of sovereign consciousness (or, to use its alternative name, sovereign violence) that releases a way of seeing and experiencing reality in a completely new way.

The actual empirical event associated with the chronological date "1984" centers around a three-day battle between an Indian army consisting of mainly Sikh soldiers and the militant leader Jarnail Singh Bhindranwale. It took place within the precincts of the Golden Temple complex, which houses the most sacred Sikh shrine and Sikhism's central place of pilgrimage. From June 5 to June 7 1984, buildings in the Golden Temple complex, including the Akāl Takht, were shelled by army artillery in an attempt to dislodge Bhindranwale and his supporters. To the surprise of the Indian army commanders, Bhindranwale fought back ferociously, the battle intensified, and ended with Bhindranwale's death along with key Sikh militants. Indian soldiers occupied the complex and in the morning briefly displayed Bhindranwale's body for the global news media to verify the facts: the battle was over, the Indian nation-state had won, the militants had lost etc. According to the interpretations of political administrators, media journalists, and scholars writing at the time, Bhindranwale's militant actions, his resort to violence in the name of religion (*dharam yudh*), was a self-validating example, evident to all, of the *visible failure* of subjective violence in the form of armed resistance against a legitimate nation-state. At the end of the day, Bhindranwale's armed resistance was simply subsumed into the flow of objective history authored by the state.

At first sight, interpretations and memorializations of the same event by Sikh nationalists might appear to contradict the stance of the Indian state. Consider, for example, the following sentiments commonly attributed to Sikh nationalists: Bhindranwale died a martyr's death in the line of heroic *Khālsā* tradition; Bhindranwale's last stand struck the first blow for founding a separate Sikh state called Khalistan; the Indian state destroyed the Akāl Takht and violated the sanctity of the Golden Temple complex and the

sovereignty of the Akāl Takht; in revenge for the loss of several hundred
soldiers, the army burned down the Sikh reference library, which housed
priceless Sikh manuscripts; the Indian army butchered over 4,000 innocent
pilgrims; it also violated the sanctity of Guru Arjan's martyrdom day
(June 5); the attack on the Golden Temple was evidence of Hindu imperi-
alism disguised as secular democracy; the attack was the inevitable outcome
of the Sikhs' having lost territorial sovereignty (the Sikh kingdom of Ranjit
Singh) and of poorly negotiating with the British during Partition.

In other words, the same event is interpreted completely differently by
the two protagonists, leaving the impression that Sikh nationalists and the
Indian state are radically opposed, not least in their interpretations of
violence. Whereas functionaries of the Indian state see the use of violence
as a legitimate monopoly of the state, Sikh nationalists see *their* use of
violence as justified by the memory and legacy of the Khālsā.

But it is here, when things seem so completely obvious, that it is
possible to suggest a stranger explanation: that both parties appear to
have missed the true event in the "1984" episode. Sikh nationalists and
state functionaries alike saw the episode only as an *actual* event, limited to
its situatedness in an identifiable historical moment. We see this especially
in the style of memorializations of 1984 where both parties tried almost
desperately to justify their narrative by proving the historical veracity of
events. For state functionaries, this may not be surprising given its need to
keep all discourse strictly limited to the domain of historical time. But, in
the case of Sikh nationalists, it suggests that the engine of their resistance
(namely the Khalistan ideal based on the notion of Khālsā as a proto-
nation) is, in fact, fundamentally aligned with the State-form. We see this
in the annual marches and protests against Indian embassies followed by
the ritual burnings of the Indian flag and effigies of Indira Gandhi, or the
customary idolization of Bhindranwale. By fixing their memorializations
on an actual person within the time of the present, they end up iconizing
Bhindranwale and lapsing into an idolatry of the present (secular chronological time). In this way, the hermeneutic apparatus of the nationalist
imaginary mimics the nation-state imaginary, bearing all the hallmarks of
forgetting rather than a genuine remembrance of the Khālsā's sovereign
violence.

Although it seems counterintuitive, this forgetting is largely the result of a fundamental miscognition of what really happened in Bhindranwale's last stand. *If*, as I have suggested above, the final act cannot either be reduced to a misguided subjective act of religious violence (as per the state interpretation), or simply elevated to the ethereal domains of Sikh martyrology (Sikh nationalism), and *if* both of these scenarios remain imprisoned within the domain of linear time, the way out of this conundrum is to ask: What is it that remains *un*actualized in this miscognition? In other words, what is the *event*-nature of Bhindranwale's act and therefore the *event*-nature of "1984"?[40]

A clue for accessing what remains unactualized can be found in the spontaneous outpourings of intense grief, pain, and rage, especially amongst diasporic Sikh communities around the world in the immediate aftermath of Operation Blue Star and the death of Bhindranwale. The spontaneity of feeling coalesced into rare shows of political unity as Sikhs from diverse backgrounds gathered in Western capitals to vent their anger. In these early days, the rawness of emotion threatened to overwhelm ordinary Sikhs' powers of imagination as words often failed to adequately express Sikh sentiment. It was a protracted moment of emotional and affective distress resulting in something close to a psychic debilitation that effectively stymied the diasporic community's interpretive capacities. This chaotic state of mind experienced by the traumatized Sikh community is captured in an art work aptly named "Nineteen Eighty Four" or "The Storming of the Golden Temple" produced by the female British-Sikh artists known as the "Singh Twins" (see Figure 5).

Michael Nijhawan gives a compelling yet critical reading of the "1984" artwork (Nijhawan, 2016). According to Nijhawan, what seems remarkable about this artwork is:

> [T]he appearance of historical actors, whose significance
> must be understood from the dominant narrative of how
> the 1984 story is told in the Sikh context. There is the

---

[40] For a sustained discussion of 'event' see my forthcoming book *Geophilosophical Encounters*.

Figure 5 "The Storming of the Golden Temple" or "1984" [Artist: The Singh Twins]

archetypal figure of eighteenth century saint-soldier Baba
Deep Singh, popularly venerated and shown in the favorite
iconographic rendition with his decapitated head placed in
the palms of his hand. Indira Gandhi, former Indian Prime
Minister, who was responsible for "Operation Blue Star"
and was later assassinated by her two Sikh bodyguards,
enters the scene on a tank. This is portrayed (like the
demon Ravana) as a five headed monster showing the
counterfeits of other political leaders, including iron-lady
Margaret Thatcher, who dominated the 1980s political scene
in Britain when the Singh Twins were coming of age. Indian
soldiers are shown brutalizing civilian pilgrims, such as the
scene in the lower left part, where a grim-faced soldier
pierces his bayonet into helpless bodies. This scene alone
resonates strongly with popularized accounts in Sikh story-
telling genres in which the mourning of the innocent civilians killed at the hand of eighteenth-century rulers is
a common trope.

Hence there are multiple temporalities of violence and
suffering encompassed in the "1984" painting . . . [I]t seems
the Singh Twins were compelled to translate Sikh suffering
into multiple registers in an attempt to highlight both the
particulars of history and the universal aspects of suffering.
(Nijhawan, 2016: 46–7)

Building on Brian Axel's work, which illustrated how state violence helped
to form the Sikh diasporic imaginary, Nijhawan shows how this artwork
presents a "reversed diasporic gaze," which produces the paradoxical effect
of creating images of violence in the "homeland" for those who did not
experience the violence and suffering "first hand" (Axel, 2005). The artwork creates an "image of mythic wholeness and emotive force" which
enables the "irruption of what has not been lived into a moment that is
lived" (Axel, 2005: 151). In this way, diasporic Sikhs are able to experience
"the inexperienceable and unimaginable" (Axel, 2005: 136). What clearly
emerges from Nijhawan's reading is a sense of the "precarious" nature of

the Sikh diasporic self that is formed in relation to the political violence of 1984 – precarious because the interpretations on which they are based fall into the "traps of dominant Western frameworks of conceptualizing" and understanding, specifically the "ontology of Judeo-Christian templates of suffering that are widely perceived as normatively shaping the public sentiments on collective suffering as universally translatable" (Nijhawan, 2016: 48).

What Nijhawan points to here corresponds to what I referred to earlier as the *unactualized*. This is the aspect of the 1984 event that limits itself only to the *actual* and by doing so fundamentally forgets the *event*-nature of the phenomena. If Nijhawan and Axel, each in their own ways, are correct, then what compels this forgetting are the "traps of dominant Western frameworks of conceptualizing" or what was referred to in Section 1 as the violence of the "juridico-symbolic" order. This point can be better explained by way of reference to the series of reflections by the philosopher Jacques Derrida on the American experience of 9/11 (Borradori, 2004: 85–137).

In a series of interviews published as "Philosophy in an Time of Terror," Jacques Derrida, writing in the aftermath of the 9/11 terrorist attacks in New York, sheds light on how to think about violent phenomena such as 9/11 or "1984" that threaten to "overwhelm not just our powers of imagination . . . but also our capacity to understand or identify phenomena in question" (Patton, 2010: 90). Specifically, Derrida points out that what makes violent phenomena such as 9/11 or 1984 *events as such*, as opposed to remaining mere phenomena, is that they rupture our "hermeneutic dimension." What gives them *event*-nature is that they inflict damage on "the conceptual, semantic, and one could even say, hermeneutic apparatus that might have allowed one to see it coming, to comprehend, interpret, describe, speak of and name 'September 11'" or, in our case, "1984" (Borradori, 2004: 93).

For Derrida, an event rises above a mere phenomenon because it contains within it the possibility of resisting and breaking with "our existing means of representation." As Paul Patton explains, "for there to be an event, we must be able to recognize, identify, interpret, or describe a given occurrence as a certain kind of event. At the same time, however, to the extent that an event is a new occurrence at a given moment in time, it must also be endowed with the *potential to resist this kind of incorporation within our existing systems of recognition, interpretation, and description.* In this sense ... every event ... carries the potential to break with the past" and to create something new (Patton, 2010: 90, emphasis added).

From this perspective, it is possible to suggest that even though the sociopolitical views of the Singh Twins and Sikh nationalists may be diametrically opposed, both remain trapped within a hermeneutic framework that compels the subject to forget the unactualized. Instead, they focus their remembrance on what is actual, or what is more conveniently visible and therefore presently at hand. In other words, they foreclose the event-nature of 1984 and refocus attention on the empirically observable phenomenon. This foreclosure is itself the result of the juridico-symbolic violence of the dominant language and the mode of reality it fosters. What remains unactualized is what has the potential to be repeated differently in future contexts, never as the same, never in the form of an identity – and this ability to repeat differently in the future is precisely what the conventional perspective makes us forget. Thus, *what lives on as the event of 1984 even as the phenomenon itself passes away instantaneously, is the sovereign violence released through Bhindranwale's death.* To some, this might sound controversial, even alarming. The alarm is perhaps due to a natural tendency to equate sovereign violence with the actual physical person Bhindranwale – whose political choices and actions remain controversial for many people and indistinguishable from those of a "terrorist." However, it is possible to look at this in a very different way. Let me illustrate this by way of three caveats that must accompany the statement underscored above.

First Caveat: Insofar as the event consists in the release of sovereign violence, it cannot be simplistically equated with Bhindranwale's actual or physical death, the destruction of his physical body, even though the latter is intrinsically part of the event. Rather, the physical process of bodily death gives rise to effects beyond its physical environment by changing relations of sense or value between things, people and institutions (Williams, 2008: 4). Such change of relations is effected through the release of sovereign violence, which can best be described as a symbolic-affective force or *intensity* (Deleuze, 1989: 294–300). As an intensity the event as such is not something corporeal or "out-there." It is incorporeal yet utterly real. About it one can only say that "*it happens*," as opposed to "this is *what* it is." One can therefore say that this event repeats differently the third scene in the *Khālsā* creation myth. In other words, the proximity between Bhindranwale's final act and the Khālsā mythos resides in the degree of intensity that marks both; a degree of intensity that is <u>experienced as the changing of an existing mindset, or, a break with an existing hermeneutic apparatus</u>. It is this intensity that was felt by ordinary Sikhs around the world and which makes the matrix of the State-form quake (for an infinitesimal moment) as the State's sovereignty is made to clash with nonstate sovereignties, breaking the illusion of a single sovereignty.

Second Caveat: The release of sovereign violence happens simultaneously with the *becoming visible* of the hermeneutic apparatus itself, which is none other than the state apparatus in all its glory – administrative, mediatic, and academic. The effect of releasing sovereign violence is that it exposes the illusion of the Indian state as a secular entity and makes it appear as what it actually is: an ethno-religious state (Singh, 2000), or Hindu majoritarian state masquerading as secular. By making visible the illusion of Indian state sovereignty, it also makes visible the possibility of alternative sovereignties. So the event in its entirety does not occur as a set of phenomena, but as an affectively received realization.

A useful way to think about this is to consider the climactic scene in the blockbuster movie *The Matrix*. In the last scene, the cyberterrorist outlaw Neo, who becomes a figurehead for the underground resistance against the State-form called the "Matrix," sacrifices himself. In the moment of his sacrificial action, however, the ubiquitous but previously invisible Matrix suddenly becomes visible. For a fleeting instant, its spectral outlines appear, undergoes a convulsion, then becomes invisible again.

Bhindranwale's act can be seen in somewhat similar terms. For Bhindranwale's last stand against the Indian army forced the state into an autoimmune reaction against its own citizens, against an entire community, and against a sovereign institution (the Akāl Takht) which the state's secular constitution is supposed to protect. As the sovereign violence released in the act of final resistance is directed at the hermeneutic apparatus of the state, several things happen all at once.

First, the secularity of the Indian state momentarily appears in its real form as an apparatus of capture and nothing more. But in the moment of its appearance it also undergoes a convulsion. As its true form trembles the prevalent illusion of secularism as a neutral safe haven for minorities is shattered.

Second, also shattered is the illusion of secularism's pretensions to Oneness and universality. And the shattering of this illusion makes briefly visible *alternative sovereignties* that had been interdicted by the secular state's claim to absolute sovereignty.

Third, it compels an instantaneous realization of the illusion of autonomous existence and action as ordinary Sikhs awaken to the fact that they were always within the State-form matrix and never independent; that it is the matrix of the State-form which provided them with the forms of identification that are sanctioned by the state: that Sikhs are an ethnic group, world religion, race, nation etc. Ultimately, what is shattered in the Sikh mind is a belief in the protective function of the modern state and its commitment to plurality, and perhaps most importantly, that loyalty to the state was misplaced.

Third Caveat: As intensity, an event can be remembered, it can be imagined, discussed, spoken about, and it can be actualized in states of affairs. The problem arises, however, when the process of actualization, which initially fosters new relations between entities, people, and institutions, slows down and begins solidifying within a particular state of affairs. For example, during the infinitesimally brief moment that the matrix of the State-form undergoes its convulsions and is shaken to its foundations, new possibilities are suddenly opened up for Sikhs to think differently, to form alternative relationships and new political models other than those sanctioned by the state.

But the intensity of the event is too difficult to sustain as most Sikhs begin to seek the safety and comforting illusion of state sovereignty. So within days, weeks, months, or even years, the majority of Sikhs revert back to the safety of conventional structures of identity and ego gratification underpinned by the hermeneutic apparatus of the state which manages not only to survive but grows stronger as it recaptures Sikhism's sovereign violence.

For Sikh nationalists, the challenge of living according to the intensity demanded by sovereign violence (ego-loss or sovereignty-without-sovereignty) proves too demanding as it is soon discarded in favor of conventional modes of violence driven by enmity and fear. As such, the opening generated by sovereign violence is lost on the vast majority of Sikhs, whose gaze is turned back towards the familiarity of chronological time with its attachment to the present, the actual, the material, with the attendant fetishization of violence, and the cult of Bhindranwale's persona.

An important question arises here about the nature of the intensity that we can equate with a revolutionary moment. Why doesn't the intensity of this (or indeed any) revolutionary moment last? Why do those exposed to this intensity (in this case, ordinary Sikhs) fail to grasp and repeat the intensity of sovereign violence? And why does the state manage to survive its convulsions?

The simple answer is that on both sides, what is signaled by the emergence of the event (sovereign violence) is the killing of ego in the form of self-differentiation. Which is to say, the event appears only by affecting subjectivity ... it creates self-differentiation by carrying difference into the structures of the ego, which now instead of retreating into the comfort of self-identification, becomes different from itself. But this self-differentiation can never be given in chronological time (*kāl*). It can only be given as such in a time that is creative and untimely (*akāl*). Faced with this seemingly impossible challenge, namely, the challenge of retaining the untranslatability of self-differentiation, which can only be expressed in terms of the chaos of multiple temporal rhythms through the intensity of emotion, affect, desire, the ordinary person finds it easier to *translate* the chaos of temporal heterogeneity into the conventional patterns of ordinary language and thus revert to the safety of ego-identification.

Stated differently, the revolutionary moment presents the ordinary mind with a glimpse of radically different temporalities that are effectively ways of existing and forming relations with others. But for the majority the hermeneutic apparatus of the mind is overwhelmed by the seeming chaos of any "new world" and decides instead to translate the possibility of a "new lived experience of different temporal worlds into the code of a secular, disenchanted, historical time" of the present (Lim, 2010: 17). So, although the hermeneutic apparatus is briefly ruptured, and opens up new ways of inhabiting the same world, the apparatus manages to reform, and reestablish the illusion that there is only one mode of time (the present). Consequently, both sides reaffirm their faith in the present by reconstructing structures of identification as a self-enclosure. Underpinning this reversion to identity and the homogeneous time of the present is the violence of the symbolic order itself sustained by belief in the objectivity of corporeal/visible violence and the identifiability of violent actors (subjective violence exemplified either by Bhindranwale as physical defender, and state as physical attacker). By translating back into secular time, the true lesson of sovereign violence is lost.

References

Asad, Talal (2007). *On Suicide Bombing*, New York: Columbia University Press.

Axel, Brian (2001). *The Nation's Tortured Body: Violence, Representation, and the Formation of a Sikh Diaspora*, Durham, NC: Duke University Press.

Axel, Brian (2005). Diasporic Sublime: Sikh Martyrs, Internet Mediations, and the Question of the Unimaginable. *Sikh Formations*, 1 (1), 127–54.

Ballantyne, Tony (2002). *Orientalism and Race: Aryanism in the British Empire*, London: Palgrave Macmillan.

Ballantyne, Tony (2006). *Between Colonialism and Diaspora: Sikh Cultural Formations in an Imperial World*, Durham, NC: Duke University Press.

Baruah, Sanjib (2009). *Ethno-Nationalist Movements in India*, New Delhi: Oxford University Press.

Bhai Gurdās Bhalla (1962), *Varan* – Satta and Balwand, Tikki di Var (Coronation Ode), Paurī 2–3.

Bhai Gurdās Bhalla (1962). *Varan*, ed. Giani Hazara Singh, Amritsar: Khālsā Samachar.

Borradori, Giovanna (2004). *Philosophy in a Time of Terror: Dialogues with Jurgen Haberman and Jacques Derrida*, Chicago: Chicago University Press.

Cavanaugh, William (2008). *The Myth of Religious Violence*, New York: Oxford University Press.

Cavanaugh, William (2017). "Religion and Violence." In R. King, ed., *Religion, Theory, Critique: Classic and Contemporary Approaches and Methodologies*, New York: Columbia University Press, pp. 589–600.

Chakrabarty, Dipesh (2000). *Provincializing Europe: Postcolonial Thought & Historical Difference*, Princeton: Princeton University Press.

Chaturvedi, Parashuram (1952). *Uttari Bharat ki sant-parampara* [The Sant Tradition of North India], Prayag [Allahabad]: Bharati-Bhandara.

Chopra, Radhika (2013). A Museum, A Memorial, and a Martyr: Politics of Memory in the Sikh Golden Temple. *Sikh Formations*, 9 (2), 97–115.

Chopra, Radhika (2015). 1984: Disinterred Memories. *Sikh Formations*, 11 (3), 306–15.

Connolly, William E. (2005). *Pluralism*. Durham, NC: Duke University Press.

Cua Lim, Bliss (2009). *Translating Time: Cinema, the Fantastic and Temporal Critique*, Durham, NC: Duke University Press.

Cunningham, John Davey (1849). *A History of the Sikhs: From the Origins of the Nation to the Battles of the Sutlej*, London: John Murray.

Deleuze, Gilles (1989). *The Logic of Sense*, New York: Columbia University Press.

Deleuze, Gilles (1994). *Difference and Repetition*, London: Athlone Press.

Deleuze, Gilles & Guattari, Felix (1987). *A Thousand Plateaus: Capitalism and Schizophrenia*, Minneapolis: Minnesota University Press.

Deleuze, Gilles & Guattari, Felix (1994). *What is Philosophy?*, New York: Columbia University Press.

Derrida, Jacques (1992). "Force of Law: the Mystical Foundations of Authority." In D. Carlson, ed., *Deconstruction and the Possibility of Justice*, London: Routledge.

Dhavan, Purnima (2011). *When Sparrows Became Hawks: The Making of the Sikh Warrior Tradition, 1699–1799*, Oxford University Press.

Fenech, Louis (2008). *The Darbar of the Sikh Gurus*, New Delhi: Oxford University Press.

Fitzgerald, Timothy (2015). "Negative Liberty, Liberal Faith Postulates and World Disorder." In T. Stack, N. Goldenberg, & T. Fitzgerald, eds., *Religion as a Category of Governance and Sovereignty*, Leiden: Brill, pp. 248–79.

Fox, Richard (1990). *Lions of the Punjab: Culture in the Making*. Berkeley: University of California Press.

Gandhi, Mahatma (1958). *The Collected Works of Mahatma Gandhi*, Delhi: Publications Division, Ministry of Information and Broadcasting.

Gandhi, Surjit Singh (1978). *History of the Sikh Gurus*, New Delhi: Gurdās Kapur & Sons.

Grewal, Jagtar S. (1969). *Guru Nanak in Sikh History*, New Delhi: Panjab University.

Grewal, Jagtar S. (1990). *The Sikhs of the Punjab*, Cambridge: Cambridge University Press.

Grewal, Jagtar S. (1996). *The Akalis: A Short History*, Chandigarh: Punjab Studies Publications.

Grewal, Jagtar S. (1996). *Sikh Ideology, Polity and Social Order*, New Delhi: Manohar.

Grewal, Jagtar S. (2009). *The Sikhs: Ideology, Institutions and Identity*, New Delhi: Oxford University Press.

Guerlac, Susan (2006). *Thinking in Time*, New York: Cornell University Press.

Hallaq, Wael (2019). *Restating Orientalism: A Critique of Modern Knowledge*, New York: Columbia University Press.

Jaggi, Rattan Singh (1974). *Bhai Gurdās: Jivan te Rachna*, Patiala: Punjabi University.

Jakobsch, Doris (2012). *Sikhism*, Honolulu: Hawaii University Press.

Jantzen, Grace (2004). *Foundations of Violence*, London: Routledge.

Jurgensmeyer, Mark (2008). *Terror in the Mind of God: The Global Rise of Religious Violence*, Berkeley: University of California Press.

Jurgensmeyer, Mark & Mona, Sheik (2013). "A Socio-Theological Approach to Understanding Religious Violence." In M. Jerryson, M. Juergensmeyer, & M. Kitts, eds., *The Oxford Handbook of Religion and Violence*, New York: Oxford University Press, pp. 620–44.

Justaert, Kristien (2012). *Theology After Deleuze*, London: Continuum.

Kapoor, Rajiv (1986). *Sikh Separatism: The Politics of Faith*, London: Allen & Unwin.

King, Richard (1999). *Orientalism and Religion*, London: Routledge.

Koselleck, Reinhart (2002). *The Practice of Conceptual History: Timing History, Spacing Concepts*, Stanford: Stanford University Press.

Mahmood, Cynthia (1997). *Fighting for Faith and Nation: Dialogues with Sikh Militants*, Philadelphia: University of Pennsylvania Press.

Malcolm, John (1812). *Sketch of the Sikhs: A Singular Nation Who Inhabit the Provinces of the Penjab*, 1st ed., London: Murray.

Mandair, Arvind-Pal S. (2011). "Translations of Violence: Secularism and Religion-Making in Discourses of Sikh Nationalism." In M. Dressler & A. S. Mandair, eds., *Secularism and Religion Making*, New York: Oxford University Press, pp. 62–84.

Mandair, Arvind-Pal S. (2013). *Sikhism: A Guide For the Perplexed*, London: Bloomsbury.

Mann, Richard (2016). Exploring the Myths of Religion and Violence in India. *Sikh Formations*, 12 (2–3), 115–19.

McLeod, W.H. (1968). *Guru Nanak and the Sikh Religion*, Oxford: Oxford University Press.

McLeod, W.H. (1975). *The Evolution of the Sikh Community*, Oxford: Oxford University Press.

McLeod, W.H. (1984). *Textual Sources For the Study of Sikhism*, Manchester: Manchester University Press.

McLeod, W.H. (1998). *Sikhism*, Oxford: Oxford University Press.

McLeod, W.H. & Schomer, Karine (1987). *The Sants: A Study of a Devotional Tradition of North India*, New Delhi: Motilal Banarsidas.

Mignolo, Walter & Walsh, Catharine (2018). *On Decoloniality: Concepts, Analytics, Praxis*, Durham, NC: Duke University Press.

Murphy, Anne (2012). *The Materiality of the Past: History & Representation in Sikh Tradition*, New York: Oxford University Press.

Nijhawan, Michael (2016). *The Precarious Diasporas of Sikh and Ahmadiyya Generations: Violence, Memory and Agency*, New York: Palgrave Macmillan.

Patton, Paul (2006). *Deleuze and the Political*, London: Routledge.

Patton, Paul (2010). *Deleuzian Concepts: Philosophy, Colonization, Politics*, Stanford: Stanford University Press.

Pettigrew, Joyce (1995). *The Sikhs of the Punjab: Unheard Voices of State and Guerilla Violence*, London: Zed Books.

Sainapati, *Sri Gur Sobha*, ed. Ganda Singh (1996). Patiala: Punjabi University.

Sandhu, Ranbir Singh (1999). *Struggle For Justice: Speeches and Conversations of Sant Jarnail Singh Khālsā*, Dublin: Sikh Educational and Religious Foundation.

Shackle, C. & Mandair, A.S. (2005) *Teachings of the Sikh Gurus*, London: Routledge.

Shani, Giorgio (2013). "Sikh Nationalism." In P. Singh & L. Fenech, eds., *The Oxford Handbook of Sikh Studies*, New York: Oxford University Press.

Shani, Giorgio & Singh, Gurharpal (2015). Rethinking Sikh Nationalism in the Twenty-First Century. *Sikh Formations*, 11 (3), 271–82.

Singh, Ahluwalia Jasbir (1983). *Sovereignty of the Sikh Doctrine*, New Delhi: Bahri Publications.

Singh, Bhai Vir (1996). *Puratan Janamsākhī Sri Guru Nanak Dev ji*, New Delhi: Bhai Vir Singh Sahit Sadan.

Singh, Bhupinder (2014). The Five Symbols of Sikhism: Some Contemporary Issues. *Sikh Formations*, 10 (1), 105–72.

Singh, Ganda (1949). *Tuzuk-i-Jahangiri*, in *Makhiz-i-Tawarikh-i-Sikhan*, Amritsar.

Singh, Gurharpal (2000). *Ethnic Conflict in India: A Case-Study of Punjab*, New York: Macmillan.

Singh, Kirpal & Ashok, Shamsher Singh (1962/1969). *Janamsākhī Sri Guru Nanak Dev ji*. Amritsar: Sikh History Research Department, Khālsā College.

Singh, Khushwant (1966). *A History of the Sikhs*, 2 vols., Princeton: Princeton University Press.

Singh, Khushwant (1999). BBC Documentary, *The Sikhs*.

Singh, Narinder (2012). FOX NEWS Interview. August 8.

Singh, Nikky-Guninder Kaur (2005). *The Birth of the Khālsā: A Feminist Remembering of Sikh Identity*, Albany: State University of New York Press.

Singh, Pashaura (2008). *Life and Work of Guru Arjan: History, Memory and Biography in the Sikh Tradition*, New Delhi: Oxford University Press.

Singh, Pashaura (2017). Deconstructing the Punjab Crisis of 1984: Deer Hawks, and Siqdars ("Officials") as Agents of State-Sponsored Violence. *Sikh Formations*, 12 (2–3), 173–90.

Singh, Pashaura (2020). Speaking Truth to Power: Exploring Guru Nanak's Babur-vani in Light of the Baburnama. *Religions*, 11, 1–19.

Singh, Patwant (2013). *Empire of the Sikhs: The Life and Times of Maharaja Ranjit Singh*, London: Peter Owens.

Streets, Heather (2011). *Martial Races: The Military, Race and Masculinity in British Imperial Culture, 1847–1914*, Manchester: Manchester University Press.

Tatla, Darshan Singh (1999). *The Sikh Diaspora: The Search for Statehood*, London: University College London Press.

Taylor, Charles (2007). *A Secular Age*, Cambridge, MA: Harvard University Press.

Thackston, Wheeler M. (1999). *The Jahangirnama: Memoirs of Jahangir*, New York: Oxford University Press. [Translation slightly amended].

Uberoi, J.P.S. (1996). *Religion, Civil Society and the State: A Study of Sikhism*, New Delhi: Oxford University Press.

Vallee, Mickey & Shields, Rob (2012). *Demystifying Deleuze: An Introductory Assemblage of Crucial Concepts*, Ottawa, ON: Red Quill Books.

Williams, James (2008). *Gilles Deleuze's Logic of Sense: Critical Guide and Introduction*, Edinburgh: Edinburgh University Press.

Žižek, Slavoj (2008). *Violence: Six Sideways Reflections*, New York: Picador.

Zourabichvili, François (2012). *Deleuze a Philosophy of the Event: Together with the Vocabulary of Deleuze*, Edinburgh: Edinburgh University Press.

Acknowledgement

The author wishes to thank the Humanities Institute, College of Literature Arts and Sciences at the University of Michigan for a one-year fellowship from 2015 to 2016, which allowed a first draft of this Element to be composed.

For my mother, Parkash Kaur Mandair
and the memory of my father, Karnail Singh Mandair

Cambridge Elements ☰

Religion and Violence

James R. Lewis
Wuhan University

James R. Lewis is a professor at Wuhan University, and the author and editor of a number of volumes, including *The Cambridge Companion to Religion and Terrorism*.

Margo Kitts
Hawaiʻi Pacific University

Margo Kitts edits the *Journal of Religion and Violence* and is Professor and Coordinator of Religious Studies and East-West Classical Studies at Hawaiʻi Pacific University in Honolulu.

ABOUT THE SERIES

Violence motivated by religious beliefs has become all too common in the years since the 9/11 attacks. Not surprisingly, interest in the topic of religion and violence has grown substantially since then. This Elements series on *Religion and Violence* addresses this new, frontier topic in a series of ca. fifty individual Elements. Collectively, the volumes will examine a range of topics, including violence in major world religious traditions, theories of religion and violence, holy war, witch hunting, and human sacrifice, among others.

Cambridge Elements ⁼

Religion and Violence

A full series listing is available at: www.cambridge.org/ERAV

Printed in the United States
by Baker & Taylor Publisher Services